read your
future

read your
future

The Ultimate Guide to Tarot, Astrology,
the I Ching, and Other Divination
Techniques from Around the World

Jane Struthers

 St. Martin's Griffin 🜄 New York

For Bill, with much love

Acknowledgments

Many thanks to everyone who worked on this book. Thanks to everyone at
Kyle Cathie, and especially to Kyle Cathie, Caroline Taggart, Georgina Burns and
Robert Updegraff who made writing the book such an enjoyable process.
I would also like to thank my agent, Chelsey Fox, for all her help and
encouragement over the years, and my husband, Bill Martin, for his tireless
support and delicious sandwiches.

Edited by Caroline Taggart
Designed by Robert Updegraff
I Ching illustrations by Xing Liu
Oracle, palmistry and tasseomancy illustrations by Robert Updegraff
Production by Lorraine Baird and Sha Huxtable
Illustrations from Universal-Waite Tarot Deck reproduced by permission of
U.S. Games Systems, Inc., Stamford, CT 06902 USA. Copyright ©1990 by
U.S. Games Systems, Inc. Further reproduction prohibited.
Lys de France playing cards reproduced by permission of Carta Mundi, Belgium,
www.cartamundi.com.

ISBN 0-312-29148-5

First published in Great Britain by Kyle Cathie Limited under the title
Tell Your Own Fortune

First U.S. Edition: 2002

10 9 8 7 6 5 4 3 2 1

Printed in China through Colorcraft Ltd., HK.

contents

introduction

It is easy to confuse fortune telling with the concept of good and bad fortune. An ancient story tells of a farmer whose view of so-called good and bad luck contrasted vividly with that of his neighbours. One day his horse ran away and his neighbours commiserated with him on his bad luck. He corrected them, saying it was neither good nor bad luck. It was simply that his horse had run away. Several days later his horse returned with a string of other horses, and they all took up residence in the farmer's field. His neighbours rushed to congratulate him on his good fortune. Once again he disagreed, saying that it was nothing to do with good fortune. He simply had more horses now than before. Some time later, the farmer's son fell off one of the horses and broke his leg. The neighbours were sympathetic and tried to console the farmer over his bad luck. He told them that his son's broken leg was a simple fact that had no connection with good or bad luck. Then came news that the country was at war and all the young men would be sent off to fight and might even die. The neighbours once again gathered around the farmer, telling him how lucky he was to have a son who could not fight because he had a broken leg. Once again the farmer said this had nothing to do with luck. It was the current situation, no more and no less.

This story is often used in Zen Buddhist teachings to remind us to concentrate on the moment, on what is happening right this

THE SUN

minute and not to evaluate it in terms of good and bad events. It is a very potent way to live. This is also a useful attitude to adopt when using a divination technique. It is very tempting to compartmentalize the answers you get into good and bad fortune, and to be interested only in the former. You may lay out the cards for a tarot spread, not like what you see and gather them up again, telling yourself that the cards were obviously not working properly. If you see what you consider to be a more positive spread when you lay out the cards for a second time, you heave a sigh of relief. At last the cards are behaving themselves! If the cards once again seem full of doom and despondency, you may decide to forget about reading the tarot for the rest of the day and try again when you consider the cards to be more friendly. But perhaps you have missed the true message of the cards. Perhaps they carried a warning that was a reflection of your current circumstances. Perhaps later on, when faced with challenges, you might wish you had heeded their message and taken avoiding action, or at least prepared for the difficulties that lay ahead.

This raises an essential question about divination techniques. What exactly are they telling you? When you receive a message from the I Ching, tarot or the other techniques described in this book, is it cast in stone and irrevocable? Has this message robbed you of your free will (assuming you believe you had it in the first place)? Has it made you a plaything of the gods or fate? Will the event that has been foretold automatically take place? And if it does not happen, does that mean the technique, or the person using it, is at fault?

There are no right and wrong answers to these questions. In fact, there are no absolute answers to them at all. We simply do not know. However, we can postulate theories, and mine is that a divination technique acts like a mirror, reflecting the circumstances at the time of the question. If those circumstances do not change, the predictions may come true. If the predicted events do not happen, it may be because some of the circumstances altered. Perhaps the person having the reading realized that the prediction contained a warning and acted upon it. They altered one of the elements in the equation and, in doing so, changed the result. The prediction did not actually come true, but the person concerned averted a difficult outcome. At other times, the prediction may not come true because someone else involved in the situation altered the circumstances.

If you regard the techniques described in this book as mirrors to your current circumstances, you will begin to see them in a completely different light. They are no longer inflexible judges pronouncing on your fate: rather they are tools with which you can alter your life when necessary. Experiment with them to see which ones you most enjoy and which respond best to a particular problem or question. For instance, you may find the tarot is excellent at providing answers to questions about the state of your life while the pendulum gives you more practical help.

Many of the techniques in this book are so old that their origins are little more than a blur. As you work with each one, you will discover its essence and get a sense of what it is capable of revealing. Other techniques that do not appear in this book will also sharpen your awareness of what is happening to you at a particular time by reflecting it back to you. Carl Jung called them synchronicity or meaningful coincidences. For instance, you may want to refer to something in a

book and somehow open it at exactly the right page. This is a form of bibliomancy, in which you answer your question by opening a book at random and reading the first passage to which your eye is drawn. It is traditionally practised with the Bible or with a dictionary. Recently, my attention was caught by a book of Chinese proverbs on my bookshelf. I had not looked at it in years. An inner voice told me to open it and see if it gave me a message. I opened the book at a passage that said, 'Open a book and you are profited.' It was several minutes before I stopped laughing.

Once you tune into it, you will realize the universe (or you may prefer to use a term like 'God', 'angels', 'spirits' or 'other entities') is full of messages and guidance. Our ancestors used oracles in the form of birds, insects, stones, fire and other signs. These are still valid forms of prediction although many humans have lost the habit of using them. At first, listening to messages from the universe is rather like trying to tune a radio. As you turn the dial you hear faint sounds and muffled words until you finally get a clear signal. In the same way, you may think you are getting nothing but gibberish from the universe until suddenly an ordinary event gives you a message that is striking in its simplicity and clarity. It may not necessarily show you the way forward, it may simply reinforce your current state of mind. I would never have believed that a packet of crisps could contain a message from the universe until one evening when I was idly eating my way through one. I was thinking about a friend I had seen the day before and, as I did so, I took a heart-shaped crisp out of the bag. It reflected the pleasure I had felt in seeing her. Divination by crisp is just as valid as divination by tea leaves.

respecting the process

Whenever you give a reading, whether it is for you or for someone else, it is essential that you treat the process with respect. If you think the whole thing is a huge joke, you will get jokey answers. Equally, if you come to rely on a technique so much that you are unable to make any decisions without it, you will also begin to get nonsensical responses.

If you are new to a divination technique, it makes sense to practise on yourself first. This honours the process, because you are not rushing into something without any previous experience. It will take a while before you become comfortable with what you are doing and get a feel for what the technique can offer you. As you work with the different techniques in this book you will realize that each one has a particular personality and can offer you something that the other techniques do not.

When giving yourself a reading, treat it as something special. Respect it for what it is. You may find that it helps to trigger your intuition if you light candles, and it will certainly improve your concentration if you can switch on the answerphone or take the phone off the hook, so that you will not be interrupted. Write down the details of your session in a special notebook, perhaps adding notes later on about whether the predictions came true. This will help to refine your abilities because you will be taking them seriously.

If you eventually decide to give readings to other people, you must be equally respectful of them. There are many pitfalls for the unwary ego when you are cast in the role of oracle, which is what happens when someone asks you to give them a reading. One of the most important rules is to respect their right to disagree with what you are telling them. If you give enough readings you are bound to have a dissenting client sooner or later. This is not necessarily because you are wrong, so try to avoid getting drawn into an argument caused by your egotistical need to be correct and all-powerful. You may be telling someone things that they do not want to hear, so they deny them. You may be describing something that has not yet happened, so it makes no sense to the person for whom you are doing the reading.

You may be giving information that takes time to digest, and they will only do this later on when you are not there to hear them say, 'Oh! Now I understand.' And, of course, another option is that you have got it wrong, plain and simple. Everyone gets it wrong sometimes. No one is infallible and it is folly to think otherwise. I always regard it as a warning sign when someone tells me that their readings are always completely accurate, because they are probably bullying their client into agreeing with them. That client is unlikely to return.

Another trap you should try to avoid is turning the reading into a session full of doom and despondency. The tarot is particularly prone to this and many people vow never to have a tarot reading because they do not want to hear predictions of terrible disasters. If you are so disposed, you are just as likely to scare yourself with your own negative readings as to scare someone else when giving them a reading. A financial hiccup is immediately translated into a crisis verging on bankruptcy. A minor mishap becomes a life-threatening accident. A lover's tiff is seen as total heartbreak. Even if you are seriously disturbed by the tone of the reading you are giving someone, it is always better to play it down. You should always keep at the back of your mind that you may be wrong or the situation may change. Accounts of people being told by palmists that they have no future or by tarot readers that they only have two months to live are not necessarily apocryphal. Some people are misguided enough to say such things and they cause immense distress. It is one thing to give a gentle warning that the person might benefit from seeing their doctor or sorting out a financial problem, but it is irresponsible to scare the living daylights out of them.

Other people can go to the opposite extreme and make each reading so marvellously positive and propitious that it has little reality to offer. There are times when a reading is genuinely positive and upbeat, but most contain light and shade and are much more convincing as a result.

This leads on to another difficulty – assuming that you know better than the person having the reading. Someone who is unlikely to win any beauty contests may ask you about their love life, which is currently non-existent. To your amazement, you see indications of a new love on the way but, because you cannot imagine this person being considered attractive by anyone, you ignore these signs and tell them that you cannot see any impending relationships. It is very easy to make judgements about other people but do not let them interfere with your readings.

Equally, do not imagine that your chosen predictive technique will only work if you follow all the rules, such as keeping your set of dice purely for divination and never using it to play Monopoly. Two of the most successful tarot readings I have ever given took place late one Christmas night, at the kitchen table, for my brother and his wife. I was using an incomplete tarot deck made up of ordinary playing cards and pictures of the Major Arcana glued on to cardboard cut from cereal packets. The latter had been my first, makeshift tarot deck when I was fifteen, using pictures in a magazine. Because the playing cards and the Major Arcana were different sizes and thicknesses it was hard to shuffle them properly, and some of the court cards of the Minor Arcana were missing. It was hardly the perfect deck and would horrify a tarot or cartomancy purist, but it was the best I could do at the time. Using the Horoscope Spread (see page 45), I told each of them in turn that my sister-in-law would discover she was pregnant in April and have the baby in December. At the time, this seemed fanciful at best and a cruel raising of hopes at worst, yet I could only describe what the cards were telling me so unequivocally. That April, my brother telephoned to say the prediction had come true and his wife was pregnant. The baby was born that December.

Finally, try not to confuse the medium with the message. (No pun intended.) When you have a reading with the I Ching, the runes or anything else, what is giving you that reading? Is it the objects themselves, such as the runes, or you? I believe that the runes are merely inanimate objects inscribed with hieroglyphics. The tarot is a set of attractively decorated cards. In themselves, without anyone to interpret them, they are meaningless. In the same way, your television set is only a glass and plastic box until you switch it on. You are the most important element in the reading because you are the interpreter. The runes, tarot and all the other divination techniques are the tools that trigger your intuition, and allow you to give a reading. They will not be heard to speak unless you can decipher their messages. I hope this book will teach you how to do precisely that.

tarot

The tarot has a remarkable ability to focus on a particular problem and provide great insight into its possible cause and solution. It can also pinpoint future events with tremendous accuracy, describing them in remarkable detail. In essence, it is a marvellous psychological tool that enables us to understand ourselves better.

But what exactly is the tarot? It is a deck of seventy-eight cards, composed of the Major and Minor Arcana. The Major Arcana is a set of twenty-two trump cards that describe the stages we go through in life and the positions in which we find ourselves along the way. The Minor Arcana consists of fifty-six cards that have strong links with traditional playing cards. They can describe situations in more detail than the Major Arcana by showing the mundane events that make up our lives.

No one knows the precise history of the tarot. It may have originated in ancient Egypt or it may be only a few centuries old. The earliest known tarot cards were painted in the early fifteenth century for the Colleoni family in Bergamo, Italy. Later that century, B P Grimaud created the Marseilles deck, which is still popular today. Another highly influential deck, the Rider-Waite tarot, was developed in 1910 by A E Waite who worked in conjunction with the illustrator, Pamela Coleman. Waite was a member of the influential magical society, the Hermetic Order of the Golden Dawn, and his deck with its rich esoteric symbolism has been the inspiration for many of the tarot sets that have been designed since then.

The tarot has struggled to shake off its epithet of the 'Devil's picture book'. This is mostly due to the Puritan influence of the seventeenth century, which found playing cards an anathema. Incidentally, some religious sects still believe that the tarot, and every other technique described in this book for that matter, are the works of Satan. Over the centuries the tarot has also been approached with trepidation because of a combination of the startling accuracy of the tarot's predictions, some of the troubling images on the cards and its regular appearance in horror films and books. It does not help that the notorious twentieth-century British magician, Aleister Crowley, who called himself the Great Beast 666, was a devotee of the tarot and designed his own deck. Do not let any of these associations deter you from using the tarot. There is nothing sinister about it, and it can be a valuable friend that gives you guidance in good times and bad.

a few old wives' tales

Tradition dictates that your first set of tarot cards should be a gift, but this is a convention that can easily be dispensed with. Besides, this means that if no one ever gives you a set of cards you will never be able to read them. There are many other old wives' tales connected with the tarot, but few are worth considering. However, the tradition that warns against using another person's deck is worth following. If you buy a second-hand deck of cards you might find it hard to get any sense out of it, and may have to spend a long time working with it before it feels as though it belongs to you. Sometimes, you will hear this translated as a warning never to touch anyone else's cards, but you can dismiss this because it means they could never give you a reading with their cards.

Another tarot myth says that you cannot give yourself a reading. This is simply not true! Many people become familiar with the tarot by giving themselves readings, and a tarot reading for yourself can be just as valuable as one you receive from someone else. What is important is maintaining your objectivity and not concentrating purely on happy, positive interpretations. If the cards contain a warning, you should listen and possibly take evasive action.

choosing a set of cards

There is such a wealth of tarot cards available that you can buy them in virtually every shape, size and style you wish. You can choose a set based on the traditional Marseilles deck or buy a pack linked to contemporary themes. The choice is yours. What counts is finding a deck with which you feel completely comfortable. If you struggle to read the titles of the cards or can never remember their meanings because their images are so confusing, you will soon stop using them.

Once you have found a set of cards that you like, it is important to familiarize yourself with them. Spend plenty of time looking at each card in turn, listening carefully to what your intuition tells you about it. Jot down these ideas, preferably in a special notebook, because they will help you to elaborate on the meanings of the cards. Make sure the cards become thoroughly jumbled up before you use them, otherwise your layouts will merely follow the running order of the tarot rather than giving a proper reading.

If you wish, you can sleep with the cards under your pillow before using them, to impregnate them with your energy. However, this is entirely a matter of choice. You can also follow tradition by wrapping your cards in a piece of purple silk between readings and storing them in a wooden box facing the east. Some people believe this protects the cards from harmful influences but, once again, the choice is yours.

giving a tarot reading

If you are a tarot novice, you are probably counting the minutes until you can give your first reading. However, you will feel more relaxed, and the reading will be more powerful, if you have learned the basic meaning of each card and do not have to keep referring to this or any other book. Readings that are regularly punctuated by frantic searches through a book are rarely a comfortable or satisfying experience. Once you have mastered the essential meaning of each card, you can use your intuition to flesh out your interpretation.

As with every other technique in this book, it is essential that you do not dramatize your reading with dire prognostications. Even if you are privately alarmed by the gloomy nature of the cards in a reading, you should not convey this to the other person. People have been put in fear of their lives by unprofessional tarot readers who are more interested in fostering their sense of power than in giving responsible readings. Always remember the golden rule – the events and situations shown in the reading may not happen. You may also have to reassure the questioner (the recipient of the reading) about the images on some of the cards, which can be disturbing if not fully understood. For instance, it is a common reaction to the Death card to imagine that it indicates a physical death, whereas the card actually refers to profound psychological changes.

The instructions that follow describe how to give someone a reading. You follow exactly the same process if you want to read the cards for yourself. Ask the questioner to shuffle the cards well while thinking of the question they want the cards to answer. When they are ready they can either immediately hand the cards to you, or follow tradition and cut them into three piles and rebuild the deck before handing it over. Again, it depends whether you want to be traditional. You then deal the cards out into one of the layouts described later in this chapter. Alternatively, you can fan the cards out on the table in front of you and ask the questioner to pick the requisite number for the layout. You place the first card they choose in the first position, the second in the second position, and so on. You are then ready to read the cards. Take note of any cards that fall out of the deck while it is being shuffled or make their presence felt in some other way. When a card behaves like this it often encapsulates the nature of the question with astonishing accuracy, sometimes even humorously. It is as though the tarot is reminding us of the purpose of the reading.

Before you launch into your reading, study the cards to gain an initial impression of the spread. Is there a predominance of one suit from the Minor Arcana? If so, the nature of that suit will show the general tenor of the reading (see the Minor Arcana section for more details). Is there an above-average number of cards from the Major Arcana (higher than a ratio of three Major Arcana cards to every seven from the Minor Arcana)? This will suggest that the subject of the reading may be out of the questioner's hands to a large extent. Are there several court cards? This means a lot of people are involved in the situation that the cards describe, or they are trying to influence the questioner in some way.

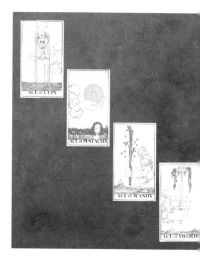

Aces describe new beginnings, so several aces in a spread can mean big changes.

Sometimes the tarot does not answer the question it has been asked. Instead, it concentrates on something completely different. For instance, your question about a relationship may remain unanswered because the cards are describing your health or your job prospects. This is not a reflection of the competence, or otherwise, of the tarot reader – it simply means that specific areas of your life need to be examined and the tarot is drawing your attention to them. As you become an accomplished tarot reader you will also recognize that on rare occasions the cards refuse to make any sense, and you cannot give a coherent reading. This may be because the time is not right for a reading. This can be frustrating but you must learn to respect the tarot in all its moods, even when it is being unco-operative.

major or minor?

Some people prefer to work with only the Major Arcana and to ignore the Minor Arcana. Although some spreads are designed for sole use with the Major Arcana, most benefit from using the Minor Arcana as well. The combination of the two gives a much richer and more detailed reading, with more light and shade.

reversed cards

During the course of shuffling and laying out the cards, it is almost inevitable that some of them will be reversed, or turned the wrong way round. It is up to you whether you give these reversed cards a separate interpretation from their upright position, or simply turn them round and read them as normal. You may prefer to use only the upright meanings when you are learning to read the tarot, because that is quite enough information to remember at first, and then give reversed meanings when you are more proficient. Having said that, many professional tarot readers dispense with reversed meanings altogether. This has no bearing on their level of expertise – it is purely a matter of personal preference. Reversed meanings are not given here – the interpretation of each card includes its possible reversed meaning. Let your intuition dictate which parts of each interpretation you focus on.

significators

A significator is a tarot card, taken from the court cards of the Minor Arcana, that represents the questioner. Although you do not have to use a significator, it is helpful to choose one in case it appears in your reading, when it gives additional information or added significance to the position in which it falls.

To choosing a significator, select the relevant suit by linking it to the personality of your questioner, as described in the individual interpretations of the court cards, or their Sun sign. Wands rule the Fire signs of Aries, Leo and Sagittarius, Pentacles the Earth signs of Taurus, Virgo and Capricorn, Swords the Air signs of Gemini, Libra and Aquarius and Cups the Water signs of Cancer, Scorpio and Pisces. Choose a Knight for an adolescent, a Queen for a woman and a King for a man.

the major arcana

These twenty-two cards are also known as the trump cards. They show man's journey through life and are believed to reflect the twenty-two paths of the cabbalist Tree of Life, and also to reflect Jung's archetypes. Drawing parallels with such concepts is beyond the scope of this book, but they are fascinating avenues to explore if you are interested in discovering the links between the different esoteric traditions. The cards illustrated in this chapter belong to the Universal Rider-Waite deck, a more brightly coloured version of the original Rider-Waite deck. Each card contains a wealth of images that echo its meaning and will trigger your intuition.

0 The Fool

In many decks the Fool is unnumbered because it forms both the start and finish of the sequence of Major Arcana cards. This is the card of beginnings, which are usually embarked upon with enthusiasm, optimism and enterprise, even when other people pour scorn on them. A fresh start is being undertaken with almost childlike confidence and the firm conviction that all will be well. Very often it is, but this card warns of the dangers of overlooking potential pitfalls and obstacles. You may be so determined to step out into the unknown that you ignore the inherent problems involved in taking that path.

I The Magician

You have more power, talent and versatility than you realize. The trick is to learn how to use your abilities in the best possible way. You are being urged to combine your emotions, creativity, financial abilities and mental ingenuity, and you will soon get the chance to use them. This card is telling you to have faith in yourself. The Magician sometimes indicates that a powerful man will soon be entering your life. He is influential, and he knows it. Some form of trickery may be involved when this card appears, so be careful of anyone who is very glib or who seems deceitful, especially if you are contemplating going into business with them.

II The High Priestess

THE HIGH PRIESTESS

The main message of this card is to follow your intuition and trust your instincts. These may speak to you through dreams as well as through conscious knowledge, so you should be open to the messages the universe is giving you. The High Priestess can also refer to a period of study or learning, especially if it has spiritual connections or will introduce you to a new aspect of yourself. Alternatively, you may be about to embark on a period in which you will learn from experience. The card can also indicate that you will benefit from the advice of someone who is probably older than you.

III The Empress

THE EMPRESS

This is a card of creativity, fertility and abundance. Since creativity comes in many forms, the Empress can describe the birth of a cherished child or the dawning of an idea that will bring tremendous emotional satisfaction. If the question concerns a romantic relationship, this card suggests that it will be happy and fulfilling. It may lead to marriage or some other form of emotional commitment. This card may also refer to a house move, especially if it will bring you into closer contact with nature, perhaps through a beautiful garden or a rural setting. In the words of the twentieth-century American mythologist Joseph Campbell, the Empress is telling you to follow your bliss.

IV The Emperor

THE EMPEROR

The central meaning of this card is authority. It may be telling you that you will soon have authority and power, perhaps conferred by a job promotion or some other position of influence, or it might refer to moral authority. Alternatively, the card can refer to someone in your life who has authority over you, such as a parent or boss. They may be rather stern and dictatorial but are actually reliable and trustworthy. You know where you stand with them. If you are going through a difficult situation, this card says that you will soon have the upper hand or at least will feel more in control of the situation.

V   The Hierophant

This card occasionally represents a person, but it usually refers to a situation. When describing a person, it is someone who likes to follow convention and do things by the book. They have a wealth of experience to draw on so you might want to seek their advice if you are going through a difficult time. When referring to a situation, the Hierophant is telling you to be careful, circumspect and to play by the rules. You should not use shock tactics or do anything else to raise eyebrows. Sometimes, this card suggests that you are searching for ways to bring more spiritual meaning into your life.

VI   The Lovers

The classic meaning of this card is exactly as its title suggests – love. It may not necessarily be romantic love, but it is a very strong and fulfilling emotional bond. If this bond has recently been ruptured for some reason, perhaps through a row, this card is urging a reconciliation and suggesting that it will be successful. The other meaning of the Lovers is choice, especially if it involves a sacrifice. For instance, it might be a choice between two jobs, one of which appeals to your creativity and the other your bank balance, or it could be a choice between two lovers, one offering stability and the other excitement.

VII   The Chariot

Some form of struggle or battle is connected with this card. In order to emerge the winner, you must use your willpower and guts. This will be tiring and may involve a lot of stamina and mental endurance, but the results will be worth it. On a mundane level, the Chariot might refer to a battle to give up cigarettes or some other addiction. Or it could signify a relationship that feels more like a battlefield, perhaps a fight for what you believe is right. No matter whether you like the outcome, the Chariot suggests it will benefit everyone concerned. What it does not advocate is riding roughshod over people or imposing your will on them. You must play fair.

VIII   Strength

Draw on your strength of purpose and will – they will not fail you. This card is about beating the odds and performing difficult feats with ease. When this card appears, you may feel you are being asked to perform a Herculean task, yet you will succeed. It refers to many different types of strength, including moral courage, strength of will, sheer mental grit and physical stamina. For example, it is a favourable card for athletes who have an injury because it suggests they will recover. It therefore also indicates convalescence after an illness.

IX   The Hermit

The central theme of this card is 'Lighten our darkness'. This can mean seeking and receiving consolation from God during a difficult experience. It might represent a spiritual quest in which you look for answers to deep-seated questions and are not content with facile or run-of-the-mill responses. The Hermit can also signify a search for knowledge, such as a course of formal education or the training involved in learning a profession. As its name suggests, this card can represent a need for solitude, contemplation and reflection. It can also indicate that you do not yet know all the facts about something, and must wait patiently for them to be revealed.

X   Wheel of Fortune

This card reminds us that everything changes and nothing lasts forever. It therefore offers reassurance when times are hard because it indicates that a situation is about to alter. Current difficulties may ease, you might recover from an illness or a relationship could start to improve. Very often this change can occur on an inner level rather than through outer circumstances. For instance, you may learn to tolerate a seemingly insoluble problem by altering your attitude. Yet this card also reminds us that periods of prosperity and happiness may give way to harder times. Nothing is static – life is in a constant state of flux.

XI Justice

As its name suggests, this is the card of justice and fair play. If you are currently going through a difficult situation, Justice suggests that you will be successful provided you behave in a fair and balanced manner. A compromise might be the way forward, and at the very least you should be willing to listen to other points of view. This is an especially favourable card if you are embroiled in legal action or are considering a career in the law. It is also a good indication that a new relationship will be harmonious. If you are trying to lead a more balanced life, this card offers encouragement.

XII The Hanged Man

The Hanged Man describes being in limbo, perhaps because you are in transition between one stage of your life and the next. If so, this card counsels the need for patience and a Zen-like ability to live in the here and now, rather than focusing on the future and ignoring what your current situation may be trying to teach you. The Hanged Man can also describe the ability to view life from a different perspective, especially if that involves making a financial or material sacrifice for spiritual or moral reasons. For instance, this may mean following a vocation with poor pay but other benefits.

XIII Death

This is a card of profound change, often experienced on a psychological level. It shows that you have to end one situation before a new one can begin, and often means going right back to grass roots and starting again. The changes involved can seem radical, such as leaving a job or severing a relationship, but they will lead to fresh growth and new experiences. A chapter is ending, which may involve cutting your losses. Just as a farmer has to plough the soil before he can sow the seeds for next season's crop, so you must prepare the ground ready for new developments.

XIV   Temperance

As its name suggests, this card urges bringing more balance and moderation into your life. It may be telling you to take extra care of your health, especially if it is being jeopardized by other aspects of your life. Equally, if your life has become unbalanced, perhaps because of too much emphasis on work or a relationship, you need to introduce more harmony. It may suggest taking an objective approach to a problem. Temperance can also describe an ability to marry your spiritual and material needs so that you have a foot in each world and can move between the two.

XV   The Devil

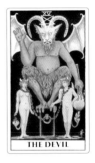

This is the card of enslavement and addiction. It describes being held in the thrall of someone or something, and feeling unable to break away. This could be a self-destructive habit, a troubled relationship, a lousy job or anything else that makes you feel imprisoned. There may even be an element of blame involved because you believe that it is all someone else's fault. However, this card indicates that there is a way out of this predicament, especially if you can understand the part you have played in it. With effort and courage, you can break this sense of bondage and set yourself free.

XVI   The Tower

Sudden and dramatic changes are on the way. They will appear to arrive out of the blue although intuitively you have sensed them coming for some time. These changes may be embarrassing or feel like a fall from grace, but you will eventually realize that they happened for a purpose. For instance, this card might symbolize a job redundancy which is a shock at the time but paves the way for a more fulfilling career. Alternatively, the Tower might describe losing face when you discover that you have been betrayed by someone, or that you had put them on a lofty pedestal from which they have fallen.

XVII   The Star

The Star is the wish card of the Major Arcana and is always a welcome sight. A dream will soon come true, an illness will end or a difficult situation will ease. This may not happen overnight, but the Star is telling you to have faith in a happy outcome. This card can also refer to something that nurtures you – a creative activity, perhaps, or a spiritual journey. If you are considering embarking on something like this, the Star indicates that it will be satisfying and well worth pursuing. Nevertheless, it may be warning you not to become completely immersed in it to the exclusion of all else.

XVIII   The Moon

This card indicates deception and an inability to see a situation in its true light. It reminds us that the landscape looks different in moonlight, and that your viewpoint may not be accurate. This may be because you are choosing to ignore the facts or because for some reason they have not been revealed to you. Therefore, the Moon may warn that someone is deceiving or tricking you, or it can suggest that you stop fooling yourself. This card can also describe a muddle or misunderstanding that needs sorting out. Sometimes, it shows that fear or a lack of confidence is holding you back.

XIX   The Sun

This is the card of creativity and fulfilment. It describes tremendous joy, elation and celebration, perhaps because of a forthcoming marriage or the birth of a child. Sometimes this card indicates that a new partnership is on the way, or that a burgeoning relationship will blossom and be very enjoyable. It can also describe the sense of sheer relief that follows the end of a crisis and indicates that a problem will be successfully resolved. If your question concerns travel, the Sun can suggest a visit, or possibly emigration, to a hot country.

XX   Judgement

Judgement is a card full of hope because it represents being given a second chance. It can also indicate a rebirth, perhaps of a belief or a relationship. It is therefore an excellent card if the question concerns a partnership rift, because it shows that the argument will be resolved and that everyone concerned will be able to put it behind them. Judgement stresses the need to stop harbouring grudges and resentments. It may also be giving you a gentle reminder that we all upset others at times, sometimes without realizing it, and that it is easy to criticize people but not so simple to behave perfectly ourselves. Perhaps someone wants you to ask for their forgiveness?

XXI   The World

The World is the last numbered card of the Major Arcana and therefore carries a sense of completion – the end of a cycle has been reached. It often shows worldly success and triumph, perhaps in your career. It can also indicate the end of one happy phase and the start of another. It may show that many possibilities are open to you. The World is also connected with travel. It can indicate a successful journey to another country, especially if it is your first visit, and is an especially favourable response if your question concerns emigration.

The Fool is the first card of the Major Arcana and the World is the last. Together, they remind us that life is a never-ending series of cycles. The end of one cycle leads to the start of another.

the minor arcana

There are four suits in the Minor Arcana – Cups, Wands, Pentacles and Swords. Each suit consists of fourteen cards because it contains four court cards in addition to ten 'pip' cards (the ace to ten of each suit), unlike conventional playing cards. This adds up to fifty-six cards. The Minor Arcana describes situations in more detail than the Major Arcana, which often provides the psychological background to a reading.

cups

Cups are the equivalent of Hearts in ordinary playing cards and are associated with the Water signs of Cancer, Scorpio and Pisces of Western astrology. Cups describe our feelings (the difficult as well as the harmonious ones), memories, creative abilities and emotional relationships. They also rule cherished possessions. If Cups outnumber any other suit in a reading, they can suggest that you are being very subjective about the situation and have a lot of emotional investment in the outcome.

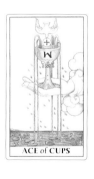

Ace of Cups

This is a very positive card, indicating the start of a situation that will be happy and satisfying. It often refers to the beginning of a love affair, an enjoyable phase in an existing relationship or the start of a creative venture. It can also indicate that a wonderful opportunity is on the way. There is a sense of communion with someone or something which will bring great fulfilment.

Two of Cups

A contract will soon be agreed. This could be a marriage contract, a business agreement or anything else that succeeds through co-operation and harmony. This is a very positive card because it shows that everyone involved will be happy with the result. If the question concerns a partnership, this card shows that it will be amicable and emotionally satisfying.

Three of Cups

This is the card of friendship and celebration. It can describe a forthcoming party or other enjoyable social event, especially if it involves close friends. For instance, it might indicate a wedding reception. The Three of Cups can also indicate the relief that follows the resolution of a problem or the end of an illness, and the feeling that one has done one's best in the face of adversity.

Four of Cups

This card represents an inability to appreciate what life has to offer. Perhaps you feel trapped in a rut, are discontented with your lot or have become so focused on one area of your life that you cannot see the bigger picture. Nevertheless, an opportunity will soon arrive, provided that you are able to recognize it. You need to look beyond your current situation.

Five of Cups

This is a difficult card, representing grief, loss and regret. Something has ended and you can only think about what you have lost. Yet you have been able to salvage something from the situation and this is what you should concentrate on. Life goes on. If this card refers to a bereavement, it may indicate that some form of emotional help or support is needed in order to cope with it.

Six of Cups

The Six of Cups has two meanings connected with the past. It can show that someone or something from the past will be valuable in the future. For instance, perhaps you should brush up an old skill because you will be able to profit from it. Alternatively, it shows a misplaced or unfounded sense of nostalgia and an unrealistic hankering for the past, which may not have been as rosy as you think.

Seven of Cups

All that glisters is not gold. You are about to be offered several opportunities but not all of them will deliver what they promise. Choose your options carefully and look beyond their immediate attractions, because what may seem splendid at first glance could entail a snag or might even fizzle out. You may have to use your intuition when choosing the best course of action. Nevertheless, one opportunity will more than live up to expectations.

Eight of Cups

An era has ended in a relationship and it is time to move on. There is an air of finality and inevitability about this – perhaps the relationship has fulfilled its purpose or come full circle, and you feel there is nothing more to be said or done. You are now ready to walk away and start something new, even though this may be painful. You know you have no option.

Nine of Cups

Happiness, stability and satisfaction are foretold by this card. A treasured ambition, dream or wish is about to be fulfilled, resulting in tremendous contentment. It is an especially favourable card if the question concerns a relationship because it indicates success. Nevertheless, the Nine of Cups counsels against becoming complacent and believing that no further effort is needed.

Ten of Cups

In emotional matters, this card is the equivalent of winning the jackpot. It symbolizes an achievement that brings wonderful happiness, particularly to family and loved ones. You will feel as though you have found the pot of gold at the end of your personal rainbow. This might be a fulfilling relationship, a happy house move, the birth of a child or anything else that makes you feel emotionally complete.

Page of Cups

This card represents a person or situation. If a person, they are young, kind, sympathetic and may have creative gifts. You benefit from knowing them, even though they may be on the periphery of your life. If this card shows a situation, it is the start of an enterprise that will be creatively satisfying or bring spiritual nourishment. It will help you to flower.

Knight of Cups

You will soon be offered an opportunity that has creative, emotional or spiritual overtones. It will mean a lot to you and could alter your life in some way, perhaps even leading to a change of residence. Alternatively, you will meet a man who is friendly and artistic but lacking the practicality to put all his ideas into action.

Queen of Cups

This woman is an earth mother. She is compassionate, considerate and enjoys taking care of people. She is also intuitive, sensitive and a natural choice for anyone needing a confidante. She may also have psychic gifts, whether or not she uses them. Nevertheless, there is an unworldly quality to her, a sense that she may be in contact with realms that are not available to everyone, nor understood by them.

King of Cups

Here is a man who is kind and thoughtful, yet who may struggle to show the softer side of his personality for some reason. He is in a position of authority but this is not always easy for him, and at times he has to navigate choppy waters. Sometimes this card advocates being more demonstrative and affectionate, especially if that makes other people feel more emotionally secure.

pentacles

This suit rules all material and worldly concerns, hence its alternative name of Coins. Pentacles describe money, investments, business deals, jobs, property, possessions and anything else of a practical nature. A preponderance of Pentacles in a reading encourages the questioner to deal with the facts and to live in the present. Pentacles are the equivalent of Diamonds in ordinary playing cards, and are linked to the Earth signs of Taurus, Virgo and Capricorn in Western astrology.

Ace of Pentacles

This card can show the start of a new business venture or anything that will be of material value. It encourages taking the initiative, being enterprising and setting new projects in motion. It can also indicate a change of career or a new job. Very often, money is shown by this card, perhaps through a pay rise, a gift or a windfall. Money can also arrive through dowries, so this card can even indicate an engagement or marriage.

Two of Pentacles

The Two of Pentacles shows a striving for balance. It describes having to perform a juggling act in order to keep afloat financially or manage your time successfully. This can be exhausting but nevertheless manageable. There may be strong connections between whatever is draining your time or energy and what is replenishing it – for instance, a demanding job that might pay well but leaves you with little spare time in which to spend your money.

Three of Pentacles

This card marks the division between the initial stages of a project and the next step. This may be a good opportunity to reflect on what you have achieved so far. It shows that the groundwork has been carried out well and more success will follow. This may involve a lot of time and effort, but the results will be worthwhile. The project is usually connected with finance, property or business.

Four of Pentacles

Everything is going well and there is nothing to worry about. This card shows financial security and possibly even prosperity. Nevertheless, it carries a warning against becoming so ensnared by materialism that you are afraid to take financial risks or move out of what may become a rut. Sometimes this card describes someone who is greedy or grasping, although they may not be dishonest.

Five of Pentacles

This card warns against becoming so bogged down in the sheer drudgery of existence that you forget to enjoy its lighter side. You may feel as though you are caught on a treadmill, or that life is such a hard grind that you can't focus beyond your next step. You may lose something precious as a result, such as your *joie de vivre*, or a relationship might suffer because you cannot spare the time for it.

Six of Pentacles

Money may be on the way. You might soon be receiving a payment, whether it is expected or a surprise. The question is how you will react – will you be grateful or will you feel that you have not received your fair share? Sometimes this card can denote a wistful envy of other people's material status or an abiding sense of impoverishment. Alternatively, it can show that you will soon be acting as someone's benefactor and generously sharing money or possessions.

Seven of Pentacles

Here is a timely reminder of all your talents. This card urges you to evaluate everything you have to offer mentally, physically and materially. It is telling you to continue to make the best use of your skills and not rest on your laurels. You may discover more than one use for your abilities. This card has links with the biblical parable about hoarding talents.

Eight of Pentacles

The Eight of Pentacles says that you have many gifts and skills at your disposal, and some of them could make you money. If you are currently looking for a more rewarding or better paid job, perhaps you could make money from a hobby. It is important to remember that everyone is unique and that we all have special skills to offer. You must continue to discover what you are capable of achieving.

Nine of Pentacles

This is a card of triumph. It shows tremendous satisfaction, happiness and justified pride in your achievements. You may have plenty of material benefits to show for all your hard work, or you might be about to acquire them. Sometimes this card indicates a house move that will be very successful or it may describe making money from gardening, agriculture or property.

Ten of Pentacles

There is a feeling of completion and of a job well done with this card. It can show that you have reached the pinnacle of worldly success or that you are experiencing a period of great abundance. Very often the Ten of Pentacles describes a happy family life. It can also indicate that a prospective house move will turn out well, or that a house sale will bring in lots of money.

Page of Pentacles

A small amount of money may be on the cards, even though it has not yet arrived. You may also hear about a forthcoming project or job that will interest you. If this card describes a person, they are reliable, efficient and practical. They can seem older than their years. Their job may be connected with finance or property.

Knight of Pentacles

There is something very solid about this card. It
often describes a situation that has reached
stalemate or become bogged down in red tape. Yet
things will soon start to move again. When this card
describes a person, they are extremely dependable
and careful, and as a result may be afraid to take
risks. This stolid approach to life can sometimes be
irritating.

Queen of Pentacles

This card shows a successful businesswoman.
Pragmatic and practical, she tolerates neither fools
nor time-wasters. She is a hard worker and enjoys
the material benefits that her work brings. Although
she may not be creative in an artistic sense, she
does have the ability to create a sense of
abundance and prosperity for herself and her
family. She could be involved in a family business.

King of Pentacles

This man is successful and contented. He may be
involved in business, in which case he enjoys plenty
of material prosperity. He is generous and
trustworthy, and people who know him would
describe him as being the salt of the earth. If this
card has a symbolic meaning, it may be advising you
to count your blessings rather than concentrate on
what you lack.

wands

This suit is linked to the Fire signs of Aries, Leo and Sagittarius in
Western astrology and corresponds to Clubs in a pack of playing
cards. Wands are associated with speculation and risk taking.
Such activities often rely on intuition, which is also ruled by this
suit. In addition, Wands rule imagination, enterprise, progress,
travel, negotiations and the ability to use words well. In addition,
they describe career aspirations, as opposed to the daily routine
of careers which is ruled by Pentacles.

Ace of Wands

Here is the birth of a new enterprise or project. It will be exciting and inspiring, and may involve either mental expansion or physical travel. If you are toying with the idea of launching a new scheme, this card provides plenty of encouragement. A holiday or long journey may also be symbolized by the Ace of Wands, which might also show the start of a spiritual quest.

Two of Wands

This is a reassuring card because it shows that you are in a good position. This is an excellent chance to take stock of what you have achieved and what still lies before you. It is an especially favourable card when the question concerns travel because it shows that plans are unfolding well. The Two of Wands can also show that an opportunity is on the horizon even though it is not yet clear what it is.

Three of Wands

'Keep up the good work' is the central message of this card. You have accomplished a great deal so far and are justified in pausing to review your achievements. Nevertheless, you still have a great deal to do and you may need to gather fresh energy and enthusiasm for the task that lies ahead. Take heart, because you are in a strong position and have done well so far.

Four of Wands

Something has been achieved after a period of hard work and it is cause for celebration. More hard work lies ahead, but in the meantime you are ready to relax and enjoy yourself. Very often, this card indicates a happy house move or the contentment that comes from putting down roots. It can also symbolize a relaxing holiday.

Five of Wands

Life feels like a struggle. You may have to jockey for position in some way, perhaps to get your ideas noticed or to be accepted in a certain role. You may also have to cope with an irritating phase in which nothing goes according to plan or you encounter lots of setbacks. There can also be a feeling of disappointment because your expectations have not lived up to reality. Perhaps you were too idealistic?

Six of Wands

Struggle and hard work have paid off and you are now enjoying the acclaim that comes from victory. You may have achieved this all by yourself or you might be part of a successful team. This is a very favourable card because it can indicate improved job prospects or some form of public status. It is a time to enjoy being in the limelight and to bask in your success.

Seven of Wands

This card indicates a difficult phase in which you have to fend off competition and rivalry. This might happen if you are one of many applicants for a job, or you may encounter competition in your current employment. Although it may be tiring trying to maintain your position, you will be inspired to strive hard and eventually succeed. One way to do this may be to add to your current skills and talents so you are one step ahead of your rivals.

Eight of Wands

Life offers plenty to keep you busy. Plans that have been in the pipeline may now be given the go-ahead, creating a sense of excitement and the need for action. Travel may also be in the offing, especially if it is a journey to a country that you have never visited before. There is a feeling of enjoyable bustle and movement with this card – things are happening quickly.

Nine of Wands

You need to maintain your current position and play a waiting game. This is not a good time for expansion, and you do not feel confident enough to take risks. You may feel hemmed in by difficult circumstances, and even doubt your ability to cope, but you will pull through. You need to draw on your strength of character and keep faith in a more positive future.

Ten of Wands

A tremendous burden threatens to overwhelm you. This could be connected with your job, a spiritual search or a current enterprise. You may feel you cannot win through or that the odds are stacked against you. However, there is a solution. Perhaps you need to delegate responsibility or ask someone for help, or maybe you are making a rod for your own back and should approach the situation from a different perspective.

Page of Wands

You are poised on the brink of an exciting new enterprise or idea. It might be a new job, a budding project or some form of spiritual development. You may also hear some interesting news soon. This card often indicates travel, be it a holiday or possibly even emigration. When this card refers to a person, they are lively, intuitive and enthusiastic.

Knight of Wands

This card describes some form of travel. It may be an exciting journey to another country, especially somewhere hot. Alternatively, it might be a house move. The Knight of Wands can also indicate visitors from abroad. If this card refers to a person, they are terrific company, a clever conversationalist and full of good ideas, even if they cannot always turn these plans into reality.

Queen of Wands

This woman is able to combine running a home with other interests. She enjoys expressing her versatility and creativity. She also has plenty of intuition which she uses in a light-hearted way. Popular and loyal, she makes a good friend and is very compassionate when necessary. Nevertheless, she is always quick to put people in their place if she thinks they have stepped out of line.

King of Wands

The King of Wands is lively, generous and warm-hearted. He also has an infectious sense of humour. He is full of innovative ideas and new plans, although many of them fall by the wayside long before they see the light of day. Despite this, he is always refreshingly enthusiastic about the next project that comes along. He may carry some form of spiritual authority, although it sits lightly on him.

swords

This suit describes the problems that we face in life. A sword is double-edged, as are the Swords in this suit. Swords rule the mind and therefore are associated with ideas, decisions and opinions. They may indicate problems that arise from the mind, such as disagreements, fears and anxieties; or they may show delays, setbacks and disappointments. Swords are linked with the Air signs of Gemini, Libra and Aquarius, and are associated with the Spades suit in playing cards.

Ace of Swords

This card shows the birth of an idea or involvement that will be completely engrossing. It may be difficult to think about much else while this period lasts. Sometimes the Ace of Swords indicates that a decision is needed, in which case you must weigh up the pros and cons very carefully. It can also denote a worry that consumes a lot of your mental energy, or an argument in which you must voice your opinions with conviction.

Two of Swords

The central meaning of this card is stalemate. You are caught in a dilemma or involved in a problem, but are unable to move forward because of a reluctance to view the situation in its true light. This may be because you are unwilling to recognize the validity of anyone else's point of view and so you resolutely stick to your guns. Alternatively, the obvious solution to the problem may scare you. You will remain trapped in this situation until you can confront your fears.

Three of Swords

Life feels bleak, probably because you have been betrayed or deceived. Although this is very painful and can make you reproach yourself for having been so trusting, you will eventually be able to move beyond the situation. Occasionally, this card indicates that a medical procedure, such as an operation or injection, is causing worry.

Four of Swords

This card advocates rest after a period of hard work and possibly adversity. It suggests that you hang up your swords for the time being and take a much-needed break before you re-enter the fray. It can describe a period of convalescence after an illness, or the recuperation that is needed after intense and strenuous effort. This is a time to relax and recharge your batteries.

Five of Swords

This is a difficult card because it describes the need to accept your limitations, whether they are physical, mental or spiritual. You may have to lose face over a difficult situation, or be prepared to walk away from something that has not worked out in the way you wanted. This might involve altering your attitude in some way, or acknowledging that your reaction was not appropriate.

Six of Swords

Difficult times will soon be over and you will feel you are moving into more peaceful waters. You are still prepared for a struggle, even though this is unlikely to occur, and may therefore feel on edge or ready for the worst. Yet your fears will soon abate. Sometimes this card indicates a literal move, such moving to a home in which you will feel happier or more secure.

Seven of Swords

There is a feeling of walking on eggshells with this card. You will have to use tact and intelligence, and choose your words carefully, if you are to emerge from a situation without damaging your reputation. This may mean playing your cards close to your chest, perhaps because you do not know who to trust. You may even have to be slightly economical with the truth at times in order to protect yourself.

Eight of Swords

You feel trapped by difficult circumstances and imagine that there is no way out because all options are barred. However, there is a solution provided you can muster the courage to see it. At the moment, your fears are holding you back, not only from escaping the situation but also from seeing it in its true light. But until you can clearly appreciate your current position you will not be able to move beyond it.

Nine of Swords

Worries and fears are hanging over you like the Sword of Damocles. These anxieties may be causing sleepless nights and an overpowering feeling of doom and gloom. Yet despite your feelings of dread, things may not be nearly as difficult and threatening as they seem. You need to face the reality of the situation rather than allowing your fears to control you. You may also be able to take constructive action that soon improves the situation.

Ten of Swords

An era has ended. The axe has fallen and you are facing the worst. There is an inevitability to this ending, but it also carries a message of hope because it is paving the way for something new to develop in its place. Once you have allowed yourself to grieve for what you have lost, you can begin to look to the future with hope and a sense of renewal.

Page of Swords

If you are about to sign a contract, agreement or letter, you should study it carefully to ensure it does not contain any mistakes, whether deliberate or accidental. You should also think things through carefully before reaching a decision. If this card represents a person, they are clever and sharp, and you may not entirely trust them. They may also be manipulative.

Knight of Swords

This card represents a situation that starts quickly and ends just as fast. Once it is over you may be left wondering what on earth it was all about, or what you let yourself in for. Alternatively, you may realize that your life has changed because of the snap decisions you made. When this card indicates a person, they are clever and successful. They are also impatient to make things happen.

Queen of Swords

This is a woman who has had her fair share of difficulties, yet she has lived through them with endurance and fortitude. She could be a widow and she probably lives alone. She takes life seriously and may have cut and dried opinions. If life has been hard for you recently, this card is telling you to take a stoical attitude and to trust that things will gradually improve. In the meantime you will learn valuable lessons through adversity.

King of Swords

When this card appears, it often suggests that you should consult an expert for a solution to your current difficulties. This might be a doctor, lawyer, priest or some other professional. Alternatively, the card can describe a man who is stern but fair and who is used to making decisions. He has a strong moral code which is reliable but not always comfortable, and a powerful air of authority.

the spreads

You can use a wide variety of tarot spreads. Some are classic spreads, and deservedly so, because they give a fully rounded answer to the question that has been asked. They include the Celtic cross and the Horoscope, both of which appear in this chapter. Lack of space precludes many spreads being shown here but you can also use the layouts given in the Cartomancy chapter (see pages 70-77).

What is important is matching the spread to your level of competence and to the nature of the question. You will only become frustrated, and possibly disenchanted, if you try to grapple with a very complicated, esoteric spread before you are ready for it. If you want the tarot to reveal all the factors involved in a situation, you will need a more comprehensive spread than one that gives a simple response. Equally, there are times when you just want a quick insight and do not need to use a complicated spread.

Once you have become familiar with the tarot, you may enjoy inventing a spread to answer a particular question if you cannot find an existing one that is suitable. However, you must resist the temptation to change the meaning of a position if you do not like the card that occupies it!

Celtic cross spread

This is one of the most famous tarot spreads, and you will see it in many variations. It is most effective when taken from the entire tarot deck, but it is acceptable to use only the Major Arcana. The Celtic Cross gives full insight into the circumstances surrounding the situation that is the focus of the question. It can also give a general understanding of what is happening in someone's life, so is a good choice when they want a reading but do not have a specific question. It is often helpful to follow this initial reading with one that concentrates on a particular theme that has been highlighted by the Celtic Cross.

The spread shown here is for Rosemary, who wanted to know whether to pursue her interest in healing. She was worried that it would be difficult to combine it with her busy career, not only financially but also in terms of managing her time.

Of the three Major Arcana cards that appear in the spread, two of them refer to Rosemary's future, which indicates that this will have an important influence. The fact that there is only one court card shows that the decision rests entirely in Rosemary's hands. There are four Swords, showing that she has been thinking a lot about the question and possibly even worrying about it. Notice how the messages of the cards reflect the nature of the question.

card positions

1 Your current circumstances
2 Current influences
3 Future influences
4 Future events
5 Past influences
6 Past events
7 Feelings
8 Outside influences
9 Hopes and fears
10 The outcome/resolution

interpretation of the spread

1 Judgement

Things are going well for Rosemary. Her career offers her satisfaction, pleasure and the rewards for a job well done. Yet the 'second chance' message of this card shows that she wants the opportunity to develop new abilities and grow in different directions.

2 Four of Swords

This card shows that Rosemary is feeling tired after a period of very hard work, and needs to recuperate before moving on to anything else. Yet both the card and question concern healing, so Rosemary's interest in the subject is already being reflected in the spread.

3 The Hanged Man

Rosemary will soon learn to view life from a different perspective. She will find a balance between the demands of her current career and her healing work. She may also have to make a financial sacrifice in order to be of service to others.

4 The Hermit

This is the card of knowledge and insight. It shows quite clearly that Rosemary will undergo some form of training, and that this may have an esoteric or spiritual quality. This may involve retreating from the world in some way and perhaps taking on less paid work.

5 Six of Cups

This card shows that Rosemary can draw on existing skills and techniques to make money in the future. She is being encouraged to reflect on the healing work she has done in the past and the way in which she managed to combine it with her career commitments.

6 Three of Swords

Past disappointments have left Rosemary feeling betrayed and anxious. However, she must realize that these do belong to the past, and that she must learn from them and move on. Perhaps Rosemary has to work on healing herself in some way?

7 Two of Pentacles

This is a perfect reflection of Rosemary struggling to deal with her current workload. It is telling her to find a way of balancing all the demands on her time and energy, and carries the reassuring message that she will succeed.

8 Six of Swords

This card describes moving away from difficult experiences to a more tranquil phase. It echoes the anxieties shown by the Three of Swords but shows that better times are on the way. Training as a healer may give her peace of mind.

9 Two of Cups

This is a very positive card, showing the start of a partnership or a spiritual communion. It is an excellent indication that training as a healer will bring Rosemary happiness, and help her to form new associations and relationships.

10 Knight of Swords

Everything may happen a lot faster than Rosemary expects! She could meet someone who acts as a catalyst and who fires her with enthusiasm. The card also carries a warning, telling her not to rush into decisions without thinking them through carefully.

the horoscope spread

This twelve-card spread is very useful because it has a dual purpose. When used as the Horoscope Spread, each position describes a particular area of life in much the same way as a horoscope. Alternatively, the spread can describe the coming twelve months, with the first card representing the first month, the second card the second month, and so on.

The following reading was for John, who felt his life was changing in subtle ways but did not know how these changes would manifest. The high number of Major Arcana cards in the spread showed that matters were out of John's hands. He felt he was being carried along by events. The overall themes of the cards were beginnings and endings, shown by five cards – the Ace of Swords, Wheel of Fortune, Fool, Ace of Cups and Death. The High Priestess and the Moon suggest that higher forces are currently at work in John's life.

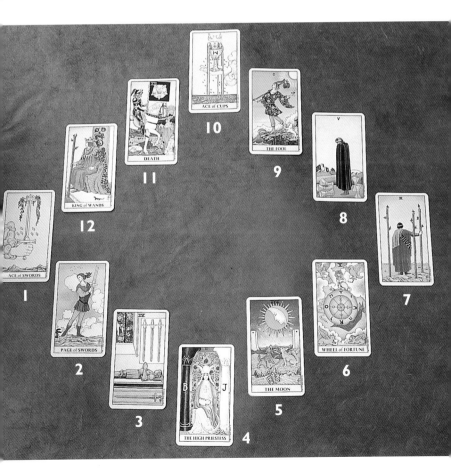

card positions

1   Personal life

2   Possessions and values

3   Communications, siblings and short journeys

4   Family, home and one's roots

5   Creativity, children, enjoyment and romantic love

6   Daily routine, work, health and being of service

7   Relationships

8   Official and joint finances, sex and death

9   Long-distance travel, challenges and education

10 Career, public reputation and long-term goals

11 Hopes, wishes and group activities

12 Secrets and fears

1   Ace of Swords

John will soon become wrapped up in a new idea or project. This will completely capture his interest. He may have to take difficult decisions as a result, in which case he needs to think things through carefully first.

2   Page of Swords

John must exercise caution when signing any official documents relating to his finances in case they contain mistakes or misinformation. He should also make a habit of reading the small print.

3   Four of Swords

It seems John could do with a rest! A short break will help him to relax. He should also strive to find a way to end a disagreement with a close member of his family.

4   The High Priestess

This card describes an intuitive woman in John's home – his wife! John is considering a house move and this card tells him to trust his gut instincts about what to do for the best. He may also do some teaching from home.

5   The Moon

Things are not quite what they seem. Something is going on under the surface, and it is connected with John's creative talents.

It also has links with intuition and therefore backs up the message of the previous card.

6 The Wheel of Fortune

Everything changes, and this card shows that John is reaching the end of one cycle and the start of another in his daily routine. It is time to change his work habits too. This card suggests that the process will happen naturally.

7 Three of Wands

John's one-to-one relationships are looking healthy at the moment. He is in a good position after a difficult phase in some of his partnerships. One relationship may benefit from some form of travel.

8 Five of Cups

This is a card of loss, connected with official and joint finances. Rather than waste time on regret, John must cut his losses, acknowledge what he has retained from the experience, and move on.

9 The Fool

This is a very exciting card in this position because it indicates pastures new. John will become involved in a new venture that some may feel is foolhardy, but which will bring him plenty of enjoyment. Is this anything to do with the Wheel of Fortune influencing his daily routine?

10 Ace of Cups

To underline the message of the previous card, the Ace of Cups shows that John will be involved in a new enterprise that brings him happiness and satisfaction. It will mean a great deal to him and may have a spiritual slant.

11 Death

The Death card is further evidence that major change is on the way. Here, it shows psychological change, and perhaps also the death of past hopes and associations. John is clearing the ground for something new to grow.

12 King of Wands

This position rules secrets and the King of Wands represents John. He does not yet know what the future holds, but he is gripped by a sense of anticipation and is content in the knowledge that events will unfold at the right time.

the horseshoe spread

This is another classic spread, this time using fewer cards. It is excellent when you want to concentrate on a specific question because it describes what has led up to it, the hidden influences surrounding it and the most likely result.

The following reading was given to Rachel, who had recently met Jimmy, an attractive, powerful man who worked abroad. She wanted to know how their relationship would develop. She was worried that plenty of other women found him attractive, and that she was not as important to him as he was to her.

While Rachel was shuffling the cards, two fell into her lap — the Fool and the Ace of Cups, suggesting the start of an enriching relationship. She took this as a good indication that her question was pertinent. When the cards were dealt out, three were Pentacles, reminding Rachel of the importance of concentrating on the present. They also indicated that this could be partly a business association and that the couple might work together. The two Knights showed that the relationship was moving steadily forwards.

card positions

1. Past influences
2. The present
3. Hidden influences
4. Obstacles
5. Outside influences
6. The best course of action
7. The outcome

1 Two of Pentacles

This shows Rachel having to juggle with a hectic life in the past. She admitted that the demands of her career had often interfered with her relationships.

2 The Emperor

Here is the man himself! The card describes his power and suggests Rachel may be putting him on a pedestal or feeling slightly intimidated by him.

3   Eight of Pentacles

There is a strong suggestion that this couple will work together.
Rachel feels they met for a purpose, and perhaps this is it.

4   Knight of Wands

This card describes the practical difficulties involved in living in
different countries. It also shows Rachel's fear that Jimmy sees her
as nothing more than one of his many friends.

5   Seven of Pentacles

The outside influences referred to in this position are work and
money, rather than an emotional rival. This is another suggestion
that perhaps Rachel and Jimmy can work together in the future.

6   The Star

Rachel should trust that everything will work out in the right
way. The omens look good for a happy and fulfilling relationship,
so Rachel should allow it to develop at its own pace.

7   Knight of Cups

Perhaps Rachel will not have to be patient for long. This card
describes new opportunities, especially when connected with
the emotions or a spiritual quest.

Tom's 'current situation' spread (see page 51)

simple spreads

You can also use simple spreads that involve only a few cards. For instance, you can deal out three cards to represent the past, present and future, or the morning, afternoon and evening of a specific day. You can also deal out the requisite number of cards to represent you, your partner and your children.

current situation spread

Here is a four-card spread that shows the current position of your love life, finances, career and health. Once you have read the four cards, you can explore a particular theme with a further reading. For instance, you may want to know more about your career with the help of the Horseshoe Spread.

This spread was for Tom, who felt he was stagnating and wanted more insight into what was happening in his life. He had particular difficulties in dealing with money and felt he never had enough of it. Although the cards offered him a challenge, he felt energized by the reading because it would help him to break through what felt like limiting patterns of behaviour.

card positions

1 Love
2 Money
3 Career
4 Health

1 Queen of Pentacles

As Tom was single at the time, he hoped that this card indicated a new relationship on the way. If so, his partner will be materially successful and may also have a lot of authority and power.

2 Six of Pentacles

This card shows that Tom must alter his attitude towards money. He will break a pattern if he stops seeing himself as someone who is always needy and begins to give as well as receive.

3 Two of Swords

Tom feels he is in a stalemate, yet is scared to break out of his current situation. This card shows that nothing will change until he can work through his current fears.

4 The Empress

Tom should be kinder to himself! It will help if he learns to relax and spends more time in the open air. He needs to get back to nature in some way.

cartomancy

Which came first, the chicken or the egg? Equally, did tarot cards precede playing cards or was it the other way round? No one knows for certain, nor does it really matter. What is important is that playing cards are a very useful tool for divination, partly because virtually every household has a deck of cards even if it does not own a set of tarot cards.

Cartomancy is the art of telling the future with playing cards and has been practised for as long as playing cards have been in existence. Many old books on fortune telling describe cartomancy in great detail, even when they omit the tarot. There is certainly something very pleasing in using ordinary, household

objects to spy into the future. They transcend their habitual purpose and become imbued with a sense of mystery.

Playing cards have existed in Europe since the thirteenth century, even though it is not certain where they came from. The rise of Puritanism in the seventeenth century did its best to stamp out what was then a burgeoning interest in playing cards. It was deemed sinful even to have a set in the house, let alone use them for gambling and divination. Even to contemplate such atrocious pursuits was believed to guarantee a hot seat in purgatory.

the deck

A set of playing cards consists of four suits of ten 'pip' cards and three court cards, which adds up to fifty-two cards. The suits are Diamonds, Hearts, Spades and Clubs, which are connected to the tarot suits of Pentacles, Cups, Swords and Wands respectively. The three court cards are the jack or knave, queen and king.

It seems that there are strong links between playing cards, astrology and the divisions of the year. There are fifty-two cards in the deck, just as there are fifty-two weeks in the year. The four suits are linked to the four seasons and the four astrological elements. Diamonds represent the Earth element (Taurus, Virgo and Capricorn); Spades are the Air element (Gemini, Libra and Aquarius); Hearts are the Water element (Cancer, Scorpio and Pisces); and Clubs are the Fire element (Aries, Leo and Sagittarius). Each suit consists of thirteen cards, which is the number of lunar months in a year. There are twelve court cards in all, and there are twelve months in a year and twelve signs of the zodiac.

Although you can easily buy decks of ordinary playing cards, there is a tremendous pleasure in using a deck that has an unusual design. You can choose from a very wide range of designs, including facsimiles of medieval cards. If you buy a deck of cards to use solely for cartomancy, remove the jokers and any other special cards before giving a reading.

Purists would say that you should keep the playing cards used for divination separate from those for recreation. This depends entirely on whether you believe the cards can be impregnated with mystical energy and will not perform well in cartomancy if they are also used for entertainment. If you do not believe in such things, there is no reason why you should not use one set for both fun and fortune telling. However, you may find that it helps to focus your mind and set the right mood if you do reserve a special deck of cards for cartomancy. You may even track down a special cartomancy deck which carries illustrations that will remind you of the meaning of each card and trigger your intuition.

shuffling the deck

When using a new set of playing cards, give them a very good shuffle to mix them up as much as possible. It may help to place them on a flat surface, swirl them around with your hands for several minutes and then riffle the deck once or twice to make sure they are thoroughly shuffled. Although some practitioners of cartomancy differentiate between cards that are upright or upside down, meanings of reversed cards are not given here so this is not something that you will have to consider.

When you are ready to read the cards for yourself, give them a thorough shuffle while thinking of the question you want to ask, and then cut them into several piles if you wish. Rebuild the deck, which is now ready to be dealt. If you are doing a reading for someone else, ask them to shuffle the cards well and cut them if they wish before handing them to you. Lay out the cards in one of the spreads given later in this chapter and interpret it according to the meanings given for the individual cards (see below). You can also use the spreads that appear in the tarot chapter (see pages 45–51). Equally, tarot cards can be used with the spreads in this chapter. Do not hesitate to blend the two techniques – you will not be breaking some mystical law! You may even discover a method that works especially well for you. As with all the other techniques in this book, once you have found your own way of working you will get the best results.

the tarot versus cartomancy

If you compare the meanings of the Minor Arcana and ordinary playing cards when these are given in separate books, you will notice some subtle discrepancies among a lot of similarities. This can be rather confusing, especially if you have embarked upon a crash course of teaching yourself both techniques. It is easy to become muddled and grind to a halt in the middle of a reading while you desperately try to remember the 'correct' interpretation for the technique you are using. This will not inspire confidence, and if you are giving a reading for someone else, that person – known as the questioner – will probably wonder if you know what you are talking about.

It is far better, because it will lead to more fluent and confident readings, to blend the meanings of the pip cards of cartomancy with the pip cards of the tarot's Minor Arcana. (The court cards do have different meanings, however, and have much more dogmatic interpretations than their fellows in the tarot.) If you follow this method, it will mean you are well on the way to mastering both the tarot and cartomancy, instead of struggling to remember which meaning belongs to which technique.

the court cards

The meanings of some of the court cards are very specific in cartomancy. Although the kings and queens describe people known to the questioner, just as they do in the tarot, they do not follow the tarot's lead in ascribing states of mind or situations to these cards. So kings represent men and queens represent women. The meaning of jacks is more subtle because they do incorporate feelings and thoughts. When jacks describe people, they are younger than the questioner and can be of either sex. They might be children or young persons, or younger partners or colleagues. Jacks can also refer to someone's thoughts or a phase that someone is going through.

Jacks have another special role in cartomancy because their meaning is altered by the cards that surround them. When a jack appears with a king or queen of a different suit, it can represent a child or teenager. When it appears with a king or queen of the same suit, it magnifies the thoughts of that person, which take on the flavour of the cards around them (see pages 58–69). For instance, when surrounded by Diamonds, the thoughts will be materialistic and connected with money. When surrounded by Clubs, the thoughts will be connected with work or speculation.

choosing a significator

	diamonds	**spades**
astrological element	earth	air
birth sign	Taurus, Virgo, Capricorn	Gemini, Libra, Aquarius
personality	imaginative, outgoing, materialistic	introverted, intelligent, objective
colouring	red or fair hair green eyes freckles, fair complexion	dark brown or black hair brown eyes dark complexion

the significator

As with the tarot, it is useful to choose a significator before giving a reading. A significator is the card that represents the questioner, and if it appears in the spread it provides extra information because it shows exactly how they are involved in the subject under discussion. If the significator appears in the middle of the layout, the questioner is in the thick of the situation. If it appears to one side, they are not so involved, perhaps because they are being objective about the situation or because it has either just begun or will soon end. You or the questioner will also learn about the quality of relationships from the suits of any court cards that appear in the reading. This is described in more detail below.

Kings are assigned to men, queens to women and jacks to young people. When choosing the correct suit for someone, you can use one of several systems. You can select the suit that matches the birth sign of the questioner. You can choose a suit that reflects the colouring of the person's face and hair, or the one that most accurately describes the questioner's personality. Rather than trying to decide which of the different systems is the most valid, choose the one that seems the most logical. If you are fascinated by human nature, you may prefer to select suits according to the questioner's personality. It really does not matter which category you use, provided you stick to it within a reading. You will become completely confused if you begin by assigning the suits to their astrological elements and then switch to identifying them by personality type later in the same reading.

hearts	clubs
water	fire
Cancer, Scorpio, Pisces	Aries, Leo, Sagittarius
creative, outgoing, affectionate	patient, loyal, introverted
white or blond hair blue or green eyes fair complexion	brown hair brown or hazel eyes ruddy complexion

relationships between the court cards

In addition to describing someone's physical appearance, the court cards also show the relationship between people in a reading. If your significator is the Queen of Diamonds, and the King of Diamonds appears in the reading, it represents whichever man is most important to you at the time. The nature of this relationship is governed by the nature of the reading, so in a reading about your career the King of Diamonds will refer to a colleague or boss, and in a reading about your love life it will denote your partner. The Jack of Diamonds would represent your child, or your thoughts, which would concern money or other practicalities.

You must also take note of the suit of the court cards appearing in a reading because that shows whether the relationship is easy or difficult. Clubs are opposed to Spades, and Hearts are opposed to Diamonds. So if your significator is the Queen of Diamonds and the King of Hearts appears in the reading, there will be tension between you. However, if the King of Spades or Clubs appeared, you would interpret him in the normal way.

the cards

Here are the meanings of each of the cards, arranged by suit. It will help to flesh out your readings if you can remember what each suit represents because this knowledge will trigger your intuition. You will then be able to elaborate with confidence on the interpretations for the cards given here.

diamonds

Diamonds are the equivalent of Pentacles in the tarot, and they rule the Earth signs of Taurus, Virgo and Capricorn. This suit governs everything connected with the material side of life – money, possessions, investments, property and one's social status. It also rules whatever the questioner values most in life, and indicates energy. Life can be very busy and lively when several Diamonds appear in a reading. However, their energetic influence is toned down when several Spades are near them. Their opposing suit is Hearts.

Ace of Diamonds

This card signals the start of a venture that will be very significant. It may bring an increase in money or it could be something offering other, less material benefits. Sometimes this card refers to a relationship in which a ring will be exchanged, which traditionally signifies an engagement or marriage.

Two of Diamonds

It is important to strike a balance in your life. Very often this card refers to the need to juggle the demands of home with your financial considerations, and this can lead to considerable tension. Although life is busy, it may be the sort of liveliness that you could do without.

Three of Diamonds

This card describes the need for hard work. You have already accomplished a great deal and you are in a good position, but you now need to move on to the next stage. Make the most of your talents and put them to practical use whenever possible.

Four of Diamonds

Although you are in a good position financially it may not feel that way. You may be concerned about protecting your resources or not spending too much. In fact, this is a very good time to consider making investments and large outlays, but you may prefer to hold on to what you have.

Five of Diamonds

This card carries a warning, telling you that you may become so wrapped up in material concerns that you run the risk of losing something you value. This might be your health if you are working round the clock, or it could be a relationship that is unable to stand the competition from your career.

Six of Diamonds

Favourable financial news is on the way. If you are currently waiting for a debt to be repaid you will soon receive it. The amount of money may not be very large but you will be pleased to have it. Sometimes the Six of Diamonds shows that you will be generous towards others.

Seven of Diamonds

You have good reason to feel proud of your achievements, but do not rest on your laurels for long because you have more to accomplish. This card warns against failing to exploit your talents to the full, perhaps through modesty or apathy.

Eight of Diamonds

You have many abilities and skills. If you are wondering how to change the direction of your career, consider earning your living from one of these talents. Another message from this card warns of the futility of measuring yourself against other people's achievements. Remember that we are all unique.

Nine of Diamonds

Prosperity and financial abundance are on the horizon. This is a very favourable card if you have recently been struggling to make ends meet. It offers encouragement if you are currently considering moving house or getting involved in a big investment.

Ten of Diamonds

This card describes the successful conclusion of a venture or activity that will bring money and material comfort. It is an excellent card when the question concerns a financial or property deal because it shows that things will go very well.

Jack of Diamonds

A busy phase, whether socially or in business. There will be plenty of comings and goings, perhaps with many short journeys or the chance to venture further afield. You may soon hear some interesting or important news. If this card appears with the King or Queen of Diamonds, it represents the thoughts of the person signified by that card.

Queen of Diamonds

The woman represented by this card is popular, vivacious and good company. Although she gives the impression of being outgoing and ebullient, she tends to keep her feelings to herself and it can be difficult for her to talk about them. Her intuition is good.

King of Diamonds

This man seems larger than life. He is an easy conversationalist with a ready wit. Although he seems to take life in his stride, this easy-going veneer hides an ambitious and determined streak. He wants to make his way in the world, even if his personal relationships suffer as a consequence.

spades

Spades are linked to Swords in the tarot. They rule the Air signs of Gemini, Libra and Aquarius. They are the most challenging of the four suits because they rule ideas, words and action, all of which often bring trouble. They also govern worries, problems, disagreements, losses, restrictions and setbacks. Nevertheless, their difficult influence is mitigated when they are surrounded by several Hearts or Clubs. Their opposing suit is Clubs.

Ace of Spades

An important decision must be made that will involve carefully weighing up your options. You may also become engrossed in a new relationship or project that will occupy a lot of time and energy. It will be difficult to think of much else.

Two of Spades

You feel caught between the devil and the deep blue sea. You are trapped in a stalemate and you will not be able to break free until you are prepared to look at the situation in detail. At the moment, you are allowing your fears to get the better of you. Until you can accept this you will be unable to move forward.

Three of Spades

You are facing a difficult situation. Someone will deceive or betray you, and it will hurt you deeply. Alternatively, this card can describe a surgical procedure or an injection, with a lot of fear involved. Either way, the situation will eventually lead to better times.

Four of Spades

This card describes the need for rest and recuperation after a period of hard work or extreme stress. Perhaps it is time for a holiday? If you have been ill, it is telling you that convalescence will help you to recover. Sometimes this card describes the need to end an argument with someone and establish a truce.

Five of Spades

This is a time when you need to cut your losses and walk away from an embarrassing situation, or one in which you will never win. This may involve a loss of face or a feeling that you have lost more than you have gained, but it is no use beating your head against a brick wall any longer.

Six of Spades

Life has been difficult and there has been plenty to cope with. However, you are now ready to put all this behind you and embark on a calmer chapter in your life. It will not help to brood on the past – you must concentrate on the present and learn to live with the situation as it is.

Seven of Spades

This card describes a tricky and unpleasant situation from which you must extricate yourself. It may not be easy to do this but it seems you have little choice. Beware of a possible tendency to tell yourself that the ends justify the means – you do not want to make the situation worse than it is.

Eight of Spades

You feel hemmed in by problems. This is unnerving, and you are reluctant to examine your current predicament because you are scared of what you may discover. Although it may seem that there is no way out of your current situation, a solution is closer than you think. But until you can look your fears in the face you will not make any headway.

Nine of Spades

Fears and anxieties are weighing heavily on you. You may even have reached the point where life has lost its colour and enjoyment, and it is highly likely that you are having sleepless nights over whatever is worrying you. However, most of your fears are imaginary and the situation is not as dire as it seems.

Ten of Spades

This is one of the most difficult cards in the deck because it shows that you have reached rock bottom. An unpleasant situation may have reached a climax or your worst fears may have been realized. Although the picture seems bleak, you have reached a turning point. From now on, the only way to go is up.

Jack of Spades

Be careful about who you trust. Someone is not as reliable or honest as they seem. This may be unintentional, although there is a chance that you are deliberately being misled. If you have to sign a contract or agreement, make sure you read the small print. Check it, too, for obvious omissions. If you have a secret, it will be wise to keep it to yourself for the time being.

Queen of Spades

The woman described by this card is emotionally reserved, and it can be difficult to get close to her. This is because life has not been kind to her, and her natural reaction has been to keep herself to herself. Yet her emotions may run deeper than she cares to admit. Occasionally, this card can indicate a woman who is spiteful or who makes mischief.

King of Spades

This man is successful, influential and respected. He has a good career, possibly in politics, the law or medicine. He is a strategist with a cool head, and can be rather aloof. Although he is faithful and reliable, he is not openly affectionate. There is a chance that he can be jealous.

hearts

This is considered to be the most favourable suit. It is the equivalent of Cups in the tarot and is associated with the Water signs of Cancer, Scorpio and Pisces. It rules all matters of the heart, including relationships, friendships and the affection that fuels them. Hearts also have a very creative aspect and are linked with abundance and artistic abilities. They cheer up any spread because they always refer to joy and love, so have a balancing effect on difficult cards. Their opposing suit is Diamonds.

Ace of Hearts

This is a marvellous card for relationships because it shows that a new partnership is on the way or that an existing alliance will enter an enjoyable phase. For instance, you might fall in love with your current partner all over again. It can also indicate a new creative or artistic enterprise.

Two of Hearts

A contract or agreement will soon be signed. It might be a financial agreement but could equally be a marriage licence. Whatever the nature of the agreement, it will bring happiness and contentment. This card also shows the desire to form a close relationship.

Three of Hearts

This is a card of celebration. It can describe a celebration to which many people are invited, such as a wedding or birthday party, or a more private celebration, perhaps to welcome the end of a difficult phase. The Three of Hearts can also signify the joys of friendship.

Four of Hearts

You are feeling stale. Life has lost its exciting edge. This may be because your routine leaves a lot to be desired. Occasionally, it can also be because you have everything you need and nothing to aim for. An opportunity will soon arrive to liven things up, provided you notice it when it appears.

Five of Hearts

This difficult card describes loss and regret. Very often, this is connected with a broken relationship, or something else that you valued which has come to an end. However, there is nothing to be gained from crying over spilt milk. You must concentrate on what you have salvaged and learned from the experience, not what you have lost.

Six of Hearts

Something or someone from the past is important. It might be an old skill or talent that will stand you in good stead in the future, and which is worth relearning. Alternatively, it describes someone from your past who will reappear and be helpful.

Seven of Hearts

This is one of the most favourable cards in the entire deck. It describes a wealth of opportunities awaiting you. However, not all of them will deliver what they promise, and some may be too good to be true. The opportunity that turns out to be most favourable is unlikely to seem that way at first.

Eight of Hearts

Although this card describes the end of a relationship, it carries an air of resignation rather than regret. You know that, despite having put your best efforts into this partnership, it has reached the end of the road. There is nothing more you can do, and there is no point in wasting time trying to salvage something that is obviously over.

Nine of Hearts

Here is the wish card! It promises that a treasured wish or hope will come true. This may concern a relationship, a creative venture or anything else that you value greatly. If your question concerns moving house, it suggests that you will be happy in your new home.

Ten of Hearts

This is a most favourable card, indicating a very happy and contented phase in your life. It often describes the culmination of something that will bring joy, such as a house move, a new chapter in a relationship or the attainment of anything else that gives you satisfaction and contentment.

Jack of Hearts

This card represents Cupid, so love may be on the horizon. However, other Hearts cards, such as the Ace or Two, will be needed to support this suggestion. This card can symbolize your lover or best friend, and it can also represent someone's affectionate thoughts about you.

Queen of Hearts

This card describes a woman who is affectionate, demonstrative and emotional. She is creative, sensitive and something of an earth mother. She enjoys having people around her and taking care of them. The Queen of Hearts can also describe a significant emotional relationship with a man or woman.

King of Hearts

The man described by this card is a real heart-throb! He is probably handsome, affectionate, charming and sensitive. However, his many social skills and attractive appearance hide a shy and somewhat moody side. He needs some time to himself every so often, and his partner must respect and understand this.

clubs

This suit is the equivalent of Wands in the tarot and relates to the Fire signs of Aries, Leo and Sagittarius. Clubs rule travel, negotiations, business matters, ambition, speculation and one's progress through life. They also govern the ability to be clever with words. They rule organizations, societies and other group activities, in all of which it is helpful to be able to get on well with everyone else involved. Their opposing suit is Spades.

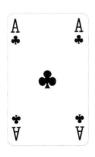

Ace of Clubs

This is the start of a marvellously exciting phase in your life, especially if it is associated with the birth of a new idea or project. It is also an excellent time to take the initiative and make the most of the opportunities that come along. You have a lot to look forward to!

Two of Clubs

You are in a strong position, and it may even be a better one than you currently realize. This is a very good time to seize opportunities that will consolidate your present situation. Modest gambles connected with negotiations or business deals will pay off, provided you do not over-reach yourself.

Three of Clubs

Everything is going well, and you have good reason to feel confident about the outcome. This is a very favourable card if you are involved in a business deal or some form of speculation. You have made an excellent start and are in a good position to enjoy further success.

Four of Clubs

Recent efforts have paid off and you are now reaping the rewards. Although the work is not over yet, you are justified in enjoying a minor celebration. This card frequently describes a successful house move or property deal, and can also represent a relaxing holiday.

Five of Clubs

Prepare for plenty of irritating delays, minor mishaps and a general feeling that nothing is going the way you expected. These setbacks are not serious but they will test your strength of character. They may also mean you have to think on your feet or invent some clever excuses to explain away the problems.

Six of Clubs

This card describes a successful endeavour and the chance to rest on your laurels temporarily. This may happen when you have completed one phase in a business deal and have yet to become involved in the next. At the moment, you are enjoying the praise and congratulations of your peers or colleagues.

Seven of Clubs

You are slightly unsure of your ground and feel that you have to hustle or fight off a lot of competition. This is tiring, but you must keep your wits about you. Provided you muster your willpower and determination, you will eventually be victorious.

Eight of Clubs

This is a very busy phase, especially where travel and work are concerned. There is certainly never a dull moment and you feel as though everything is speeded up. Decisions are taken swiftly, opportunities appear to arise out of thin air and you are fully occupied in keeping up with the latest developments.

Nine of Clubs

This is not a good time to expand or take risks. It is far wiser to consolidate your current assets, conserve your energy and wait for a more favourable time to move ahead. You may feel rather defensive about your position, but do not alarm yourself with groundless fears.

Ten of Clubs

Something is weighing heavily on you and it feels like a hefty burden. You are struggling to cope, and feel that you have taken on too much. Yet there is a solution which may involve delegating some of your work, organizing your time more efficiently or admitting defeat over something.

Jack of Clubs

The Jack of Clubs can represent a close friend or someone who will support you. It can also describe some form of conversation, whether it is an enjoyable gossip or a serious business discussion. When it appears with the King or Queen of Clubs, it represents the thoughts of the person described by that card.

Queen of Clubs

This woman is probably involved in business, in which case she will be successful at it. She is certainly businesslike, organized and practical. She is also popular, intelligent and clever with words. She appreciates all the good things that money can buy, and does not stint herself.

King of Clubs

This man is practical, efficient and reliable. He is so capable that he is the first person you would turn to in a crisis, whether in a professional capacity or as a staunch friend. He is good at handling money, and takes pride in providing for his family. He enjoys a comfortable standard of living.

combinations of cards

In cartomancy, two or more cards of a particular value have a special meaning. They give your reading extra depth and interest. Here is a selection of these combinations. As you become more familiar with reading cards you may be able to elaborate on these and add others that you have noticed yourself.

sevens
two	An enjoyable time.
three	A birth.
four	Be wary about who you trust.

eights
two	A short journey.
three	Difficulties at home.
four	A tricky situation.

nines
two	Modest gains.
three	Success is within your grasp.
four	A marvellous surprise.

tens
two	Big changes.
three	Powerful opposition.
four	A very successful outcome.

jacks
two	Someone is dishonest.
three	Too many cooks spoil the broth.
four	Quarrels and disputes.

queens
two	A good friend.
three	A lively and sociable time.
four	Women cause gossip and possible scandal.

kings
two	A friend or business partner.
three	Business achievements.
four	Acclaim, good fortune and success.

aces
two	Important beginnings.
three	A marvellous opportunity.
four	Radical change.

the spreads

Several cartomancy spreads or layouts are given here to answer a variety of questions. With each one you deal out the cards in a particular pattern to discover the answer to your question. You can also use the spreads in the tarot chapter. If you want to ask a particular question and cannot find a suitable spread, there is nothing to stop you inventing your own. Think about the categories you wish to include in your spread, ensuring that they explain the question in the way you want. Then note which position represents which category – so that you are not tempted to change your mind if you do not like the way the cards fall – and deal out the spread.

Many traditional cartomancy spreads are complicated, but the ones given in this chapter are relatively simple and suitable for beginners. Yet they also provide enough information to be valuable to accomplished cartomancers.

the wish spread

This is a classic way to discover whether your wish will be granted. It does not involve interpreting the cards themselves – you simply deal out five piles of cards and see which card contains the Nine of Hearts, which is the wish card in cartomancy.

Decide which card, known as the significator, represents you. If you are reading the cards for someone else, choose the card that best represents them. Find it in the deck and put it to one side. Then shuffle the cards while thinking of your wish. When you are ready, deal out four cards in a straight line, leaving a gap between cards two and three. Place the significator, face up, in this gap. Now deal the rest of the cards into the five piles, working systematically from left to right. Note that piles one and two will each have eleven cards, while the other three will have only ten.

When all the cards have been dealt, look through each pile in turn for the Nine of Hearts. Begin with the middle pile containing the significator. If the Nine of Hearts is in this pile, it is a very favourable sign and your wish will be granted. If the card is

not in the significator's pile, look for it in the first pile. If it is here, your wish will be granted after a short delay. If you find the Nine of Hearts in the second pile, your wish will be partly granted. If you find it in the third pile, your wish is unlikely to come true. If it is in the fourth pile, your wish will bring trouble and you are advised to think again.

the Bohemian spread

This is a classic layout using seven cards. It is a good spread for a beginner because it is not too complicated, and the categories are easy to interpret. Choose a significator in the usual way but keep the card in the deck. Shuffle the cards well and then deal them out in the pattern shown here.

Amanda wanted to know whether to stay in her current job in the hope of being promoted or to accept the better paid job she had been offered by another company. She felt her hands were slightly tied because she was strongly attracted to her boss and wanted to stay with him. Yet she felt she was stagnating in her current position. Her significator was the Queen of Spades, chosen because she is a Libran.

card positions

1 Your current circumstances
2 Your current influences
3 Your relationships
4 Your hopes and wishes
5 What is unexpected
6 Immediate events
7 Favourable influences

I Two of Clubs

This card offers reassurance because it tells Amanda that she may be in a better position than she realizes. Careful gambles will pay off, although she should not do anything reckless.

2   Six of Diamonds

Money is on the way for Amanda, provided she is prepared to look for it. This card tells her that she is quite capable of earning more money from the other job, should she decide to accept it.

3   Jack of Diamonds

Amanda will soon embark on a very busy phase in which she meets many more people through her work. Perhaps one of them will be someone who takes her mind off her boss?

4   Four of Hearts

This card underlines Amanda's current boredom and sense that she is not making any headway. It also carries a slight warning not to lose sight of what is important, which might result in missing some good opportunities.

5   Jack of Hearts

Here is Cupid! An unexpected romance will soon brighten up Amanda's life considerably. The question is whether it will be with her boss or someone else. As this position rules what is unexpected, the relationship will probably be either with someone Amanda has yet to meet or with someone she knows but has not considered as a prospective partner.

6   Ace of Clubs

The pace of life is going to pick up considerably for Amanda. Boredom will be a thing of the past and she may even struggle to find enough hours in the day to fit in all the activities that are coming her way.

7   Eight of Diamonds

One of the meanings of this card is a change of career, so it looks as though Amanda will be switching jobs after all. This suggests that her new romance will not be with her boss. She will be able to move ahead with excitement and the chance of developing her talents in new ways.

the options spread

This is an excellent spread to use when you are faced with a choice, because it describes the background and outcome of each of the choices you are considering. You can expand the spread to include more choices if necessary, by dealing out an extra card in each category to represent each choice. In this way, card number three would represent the background influence for option three, card number four would represent the current circumstances of option one, and so on. In other words, you deal out each card for the background influences row before dealing out the cards for the current circumstances row.

Amanda wanted to use this spread to look more clearly at what she saw as her two choices – remaining in her current job (option one) or looking for something new (option two). The positive results of this reading made her decide to accept the new job.

card positions

1 Background influence for option 1
2 Background influence for option 2
3 Current circumstances of option 1
4 Current circumstances of option 2
5 What is against you for option 1
6 What is against you for option 2
7 What is in your favour for option 1
8 What is in your favour for option 2
9 Outcome of option 1
10 Outcome of option 2

1 Eight of Spades

Amanda had been reluctant to look at her life in too much detail in case she did not like what she saw. This included her on-off relationship with her boss. She had not wanted to admit to herself that it might be a non-starter.

2 Six of Clubs

The company that would like to employ Amanda has chosen her because of her excellent track record, which is reflected in this card. It represents success and the acclaim of one's peers.

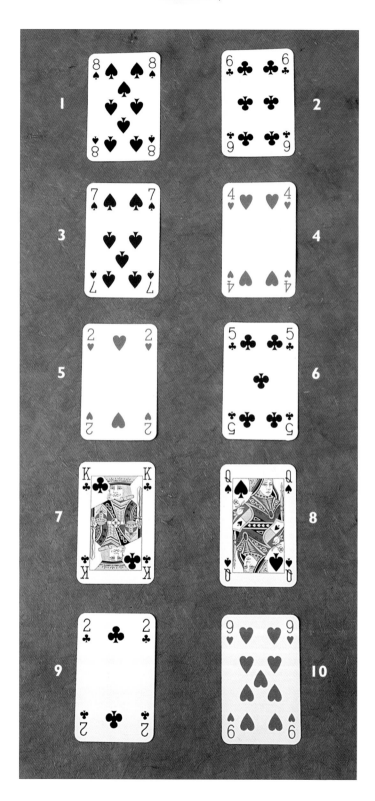

3 Seven of Spades

This is a difficult card and its position here suggests that Amanda's current job is causing more problems or heartache than she is prepared to admit.

4 Four of Hearts

Although the prospect of the new job does not fill Amanda with excitement at the moment, this card suggests that it will turn out to be a marvellous opportunity if she is prepared to give it a chance.

5 Two of Hearts

Here is the nub of the problem. This card describes happy partnerships, and refers to Amanda's reluctance to leave her current job because of her strong attraction to her boss. She feels powerfully connected to him.

6 Five of Clubs

There will be some irritating delays and minor setbacks involved in taking up the new job, but they are nothing to worry about and will soon be sorted out.

7 King of Clubs

This card represents Amanda's boss because it describes a businessman. Clubs are the opposing suit to Spades, which is Amanda's suit, indicating that the relationship between them is not easy.

8 Queen of Spades

Here is Amanda's significator, showing that it will definitely be in her favour to take the new job. She will be in a good position and will come into her own.

9 Two of Clubs

Amanda will be in a good position if she stays in her current job but she will have to work very hard if she is to get any further. There may not be many opportunities for further growth.

10 Nine of Hearts

This is the wish card, showing that accepting the new job will bring many opportunities and much happiness. Some of her wishes will come true. This card is saying a definite 'yes' to the job offer.

dice

There is nothing new about dice. Legend has it that when Julius Caesar decided to take his army across the Rubicon he said, 'iacta alea est' – 'the die is cast'. It is not known when dice were invented, but they are believed to date back to ancient Asia at the very least.

Originally, dice were made from the knucklebones of animals and were used for divination. These dice had four faces. In time, dice were created from almost anything people could get their hands on, from fruit stones to teeth. In ancient Greece, dice had six sides and most were fashioned from bone and ivory, although some were made from metals and semi-precious stones. Gambling was highly popular at that time, using two or three dice. When using three dice, the highest throw (three sixes) was called Aphrodite, and the lowest (three ones) the dog.

It is highly likely that humans have always used dice for divination, just as we have used many other objects to tell the future. Interestingly enough, we seem to have invented dice for cheating at the same time! Loaded dice and those with shaved sides to alter the way they land have been found in ancient burial sites in Asia, Egypt and North and South America.

As with many other ancient forms of divination, there are several rules associated with throwing dice. However, it is entirely a matter of personal choice whether these are followed or ignored. Many of these rules are arbitrary and were probably developed to add mystery and significance to divination by dice. Do not be afraid to develop your own guidelines, nor to be completely spontaneous, using the dice in different ways according to your instincts at the time. Trusting your instincts is the best way to get a good reading. Slavishly following a set of pronouncements, when you see no good reason for them, is likely to restrict your intuition and therefore reduce the accuracy of your readings.

Classic divination with dice involves throwing three dice into a chalk circle that you have drawn, approximately 12in (30cm) in diameter. You then add up the total number of spots on the dice that fall within the circle and interpret them accordingly. For instance, if you throw a three, two and five, the total is ten. This is

These three dice add up to eleven, indicating a temporary separation from someone.

the number to look up in the list of interpretations below. Any dice that fall outside the circle are treated in one of two ways. You can either ignore them or add up the number of spots and interpret their total. If all three dice fall outside the circle, you should gather them up and throw them again. If they still land outside the circle, the dice are telling you that this is not a favourable time for a reading. You may have already deduced this from the fact that the dice refuse to co-operate with you.

Tradition also states that dice should be thrown in silence, so if you want to ask them a question do so mentally. Some sources even say that when asking a personal question you should get

someone else to throw the dice for you. It has also been said that dice should never be thrown on a Monday or Wednesday, but you may believe that this is taking things too far.

You can cup the dice in your hands before throwing them or you can place them in a special container. It will certainly add to the ritual of the session if you use something like this, as will keeping the dice in a special bag, never using them for any other purpose such as games. If you enjoy using dice and get good results from them, you may wish to buy an expensive set, perhaps made from bone rather than plastic. You can even buy left- and right-handed versions, should you so wish. You might also prefer to cut out a paper circle rather than draw a chalk circle each time, or even to use a large piece of plain fabric on which you have painted a white circle.

the interpretations

It is claimed that everything predicted by the dice will come to pass within nine days. It is also said that the dice refer only to the future, never to the past or present. Once the dice have been thrown, take note of those that have landed inside the circle. Count up the number of spots on each dice because the total number will provide the source for your interpretation.

Nought

This will only occur if all three dice have landed outside the circle on both occasions that you threw them. The time is not right for asking the dice any questions.

One

You will only get this total if two of the dice fall outside the circle. It gives a resounding 'yes' to the question that has been asked. This is probably because it is so hard to get this result!

Two

This result can only be achieved when either one or two of the dice falls outside the circle. It gives a definite 'no' in response to your question. In time, you may realize that this was a blessing in disguise although it can be a disappointment at the time.

Three

Pleasant surprises, whether large or small, are on the horizon. You may also hear some unexpected good news in the near future.

Four

This is a difficult number because it means an unpleasant situation will soon take place in relation to your question. You may also have to contend with some disappointing news.

Five

Someone new will soon enter your life. This will be a happy and favourable association, and will have a big impact on you.

Sometimes such an eventuality is the last thing that you expect at the time of the reading.

Six

You will lose something that you value unless you take great care of it. Avoid taking it for granted. This may be a physical object, a position of power or a relationship.

Seven

Be very choosy about who you confide in because they may gossip about you or divulge your secrets. Seven does not give a favourable answer for business matters because it indicates a betrayal. It is not a good time to enter a partnership with anyone.

Eight

If you proceed with the situation you are asking about, you will soon be criticized. You may be blamed for everything that goes wrong, even if others are involved. Think twice about what you want to do.

Nine

This indicates a successful relationship, for you or someone you care about. It can be anything from a friendship to a marriage. If you have quarrelled with someone, there will soon be a reconciliation.

Ten

Something new is about to begin. Ten can describe a birth or the beginning of a project. It also indicates a successful time in business, possibly promotion or a favourable change of job.

Eleven

A parting will soon take place. This may be because someone physically takes leave of you, or because there will be a rift between you. It will cause you pain or sorrow, but it may be temporary.

Twelve

Good news will soon arrive. Traditionally it came through the post, but it might now take the form of e-mail or a text message on a mobile phone. If you receive a job offer you would be wise to ask someone's advice before making a decision.

Thirteen

This is an unlucky number and warns against pursuing the subject of your question. There may also be an unpleasant surprise, in which case it will not turn out to be as difficult as you feared. Sometimes this number foretells grief.

Fourteen

You will soon meet a new friend and it will be a very happy association that grows deeper over time. Occasionally, it may result in marriage or some other partnership. This person will be helpful.

Fifteen

Be careful not to break the law or do anything else that will bring retribution or trouble. This is not a good time to go against your principles or do things that will prick your conscience. Be prudent.

Sixteen

A journey or holiday will be very happy and enjoyable, though it may be unexpected. It may also have important repercussions.

Seventeen

Be prepared to change your plans, especially if you have to accommodate the needs or advice of someone who lives abroad. There may also be financial profit from a business venture.

Eighteen

This is the best combination of all. It shows that a wish will be granted. It gives a favourable answer to your question. It can also indicate prosperity, happiness and success in everything you do.

reading the dice

Annette wanted to know whether the new relationship she had just started was going to work out well. She threw a five, a two and a one, which add up to eight. This indicated that she would be criticized for something, and she admitted that her friends had questioned her choice of partner. She decided to continue with the relationship rather than worry about what others thought.

western astrology

Almost everyone knows their Sun sign but they are not always sure what it means. Our Sun sign, also known as our star sign, is the sign that the Sun occupied at the time of our birth. So if you are an Arien, the Sun was moving through Aries when you were born.

This chapter is called Western astrology because the techniques involved differ from other forms of astrology practised throughout the world. Western astrology, which is the form of astrology used when you read your horoscope in a newspaper, dates from the ancient Mesopotamians who lived about 4000 BC. They needed to compute time so they could keep track of the seasons, and their best guide was the monthly lunar cycle and the annual cycles of various stars. Their observations helped them to plan their agriculture and the general rhythm of their lives, but also took on a religious significance. The Mesopotamians worshipped the planets as deities, and they also began to use their movements for divination purposes. The rise of mathematics, combined with the study of astronomy and the use of divination, eventually led to the birth of astrology.

Until the seventeenth century, astronomy and astrology went hand in hand; there was little division between the two sciences. Both believed that the Sun revolved around the Earth, although we now know that it is the other way round. The band of sky visible from Earth is crammed with stars, and the ancients memorized their positions by grouping them into constellations. For the purposes of astronomy and astrology, they chose twelve constellations of thirty degrees each – Aries, Taurus, Gemini, Cancer, Leo, Virgo, Libra, Scorpio, Sagittarius, Capricorn, Aquarius and Pisces. They knew that the Sun moved through the twelve constellations in one solar year. By monitoring the progress of the other planets, and the Moon, the ancients discovered the length of each of their cycles. At the time, people knew the five planets that were visible to the naked eye – Mercury, Venus, Mars, Jupiter and Saturn. Uranus was discovered in 1781, Neptune in 1846 and Pluto in 1930.

No one knows why and how astrology works. All we know is that it is a symbolic language in which the movements of the planets reflect the events that happen to us. Yet that does not prevent it from being a marvellous tool that will tell us a great deal about ourselves and our futures. Although Sun sign horoscopes in newspapers can only concentrate on your birth sign, if you consult an astrologer privately they will tell you about all the other factors in your birth chart, and what they say about you. They will also give you an insight into the phase you have reached in your life and what the future holds for you. Astrologers believe that character is destiny, and that your birth chart, which shows the positions of the planets at the time of your birth, describes your character, potential, health, family life and attitude towards relationships, amongst other things.

In this chapter, you can read about the general characteristics of your Sun sign and also discover what the future will hold for you until 2010. If this whets your appetite for more, you can either consult a professional astrologer or teach yourself the fascinating science of astrology.

Aries   21 March – 20 April

element	**fire**
symbol	**ram**
planet	**Mars**
colour	**red**
gemstone	**diamond**
careers	**mechanic, armed forces, metallurgist**
day of the week	**Tuesday**
Area of the body	**head**

Aries is the first sign of the zodiac, and Ariens always like to come first in whatever they do. They are very competitive, which makes them leaders not followers. Ariens also have enormous energy, enthusiasm and vitality, all of which help them tackle new adventures and explore fresh areas. They have a pioneering and intrepid spirit that gives them an enduring zest for life, no matter how old they are.

Ariens like to drive fast and they do everything else equally quickly. They often become impatient when they think other people are dragging their feet or holding them back, and their temper will flare up quickly. However, Ariens do not believe in bearing grudges and prefer a quick tantrum before returning to normal.

This is a very hot-blooded sign and Ariens can get very passionate, both in and out of the bedroom. They are also very affectionate and loving. Ariens who are unable to express themselves emotionally and assert their independence is a very unhappy person, and will become tremendously frustrated. This is a sign that needs to keep on the move, and an Arien who feels trapped in a relationship or has a desk-bound job will soon want to break free and look for greener pastures elsewhere.

the future for Aries

2001 A great year for expanding your home and family life, but be wary about spending too much money. Even so, careful investments will pay off.

2002 A marvellous year for love and family matters. Work hard at strengthening the way you communicate with others.

2003 Unexpected events dominate. Your love life blossoms early in the year before the focus switches to improving your work and health.

2004 A bumper year for one-to-one relationships. It is also a good time to consolidate family ties and make some home improvements or move house.

2005 Your relationships flourish now, and the more effort you put into them the bigger the benefits. However, be aware of what is going on behind the scenes.

2006 Be prepared to seize the opportunities that come along, even if they do require a leap of faith. An excellent year for developing your creative talents.

2007 A very good year to concentrate on your job and long-term aims. You can make tremendous progress now, provided you are prepared to work for it.

2008 Continue the progress you made last year. Goals and ambitions are within your grasp but do not be ruthless in your drive for success.

2009   Friends and partners make it an enjoyable year, full of affection. Group activities introduce you to new contacts and provide light relief from work.

2010 A year in which you need to alternate socializing with plenty of relaxation. Be prepared to revise plans connected with your job.

Taurus   21 April – 21 May

element	**earth**
symbol	**bull**
planet	**Venus**
colour	**green**
gemstone	**emerald**
careers	**agriculture, property, beauty**
day of the week	**Friday**
area of the body	**throat**

Like the bulls that represent them, Taureans are usually placid and contented creatures. They enjoy being in beautiful surroundings and have a great affinity with nature. It takes a lot to upset a Taurean but woe betide you once you have. You would not want to be confronted by a bull charging across a field towards you, and an angry Taurean is equally daunting.

Material and emotional security are paramount for Taureans. They need to feel safe in their surroundings and need a roof over their heads. They will devote a lot of time and money to their home and go to a lot of trouble to look after their family. Taureans are traditionalists at heart and have a strong respect for convention. They can also be very reluctant to accept change and may stick with a situation long after they should have altered it. Taureans know their own minds and are not easily talked out of their opinions. Sometimes, this steadfast attitude can make them obstinate and stubborn.

Love is an essential part of life for Taureans but they have a tendency to be possessive, which can cause problems in their relationships. However, they are extremely faithful and loyal — qualities that make them dependable and trustworthy in every way. You always know where you stand with a Taurean.

the future for Taurus

2001 Your finances look good, provided you exercise a little restraint. It is an excellent year to lay the foundations for a new venture that will pay well.

2002 An excellent year for investing in bricks and mortar. Other financial enterprises will also go well, but you must be prudent and careful.

2003 A very happy year in which you will have good reason to count your blessings. Be prepared to view friends in a new and surprising light.

2004 A good year for working hard at improving your communications. You may meet someone who is very influential or who can pull strings on your behalf.

2005 Your health and job prospects look good. It is also an excellent opportunity to form a partnership, whether for business or pleasure.

2006 Concentrate on your relationships for maximum happiness. Other people will make your world go round. Do not neglect your family life.

2007 It is a marvellous year for partnerships. Your life is enhanced by the presence of loved ones. Family matters improve considerably.

2008 A very lucky year! Everything goes well and you are justified in being optimistic about your prospects. Travel and education are especially enjoyable.

2009 You need to combine work and play for maximum success. You get the chance to expand many areas of your life, including your career.

2010 A year in which many changes take place. Job prospects look good but try not to neglect your loved ones. A close relationship needs a rethink.

Gemini   22 May – 21 June

element	**air**
symbol	**twins**
planet	**Mercury**
colour	**yellow**
gemstone	**garnet**
careers	**journalism, advertising, sales**
day of the week	**Wednesday**
area of the body	**arms**

Gemini rules communications, and members of this sign are excellent communicators. They are very chatty and well-informed, and their intelligence and quick wit ensures their popularity. They enjoy keeping abreast of the latest news, whether it is local or global, and are never averse to exchanging interesting snippets of gossip. The growth in technological communications, such as computers and the Internet, was made for Geminis who adore playing with gadgets and also love being the first person in their circle to have the latest equipment.

Variety is the spice of life for Geminis, who soon feel jaded, stale and even ill when life becomes too predictable or boring. Their mental flexibility means they excel at doing several things at once and they tend to live on their nerves, especially if their busy lives mean they often miss out on decent meals. It is a rare Gemini who sticks with one partner, one home or one career throughout their life.

Emotionally, Geminis prefer to keep things light and airy. They feel threatened and swamped when confronted by powerful passions. It is often said that Geminis are fickle, and some of them certainly continue to play the field when they are in a committed relationship, but most of them are faithful if flirty.

the future for Gemini

2001 Life is starting to blossom but do not take risks that you cannot afford to lose. It is a year to consolidate your existing resources with sound investments.

2002 Despite times when things feel slow, this is a great year for laying the foundations for future success. Your stock is rising and hard work will pay off.

2003 Your life moves in a new direction. There could also be a house move. It is certainly a good year to invest in property and to broaden your family life.

2004 Control your finances otherwise it could be an expensive year! It will be very enjoyable, with big developments in your love life and creativity.

2005 New contacts lead to fresh job opportunities. Your health flourishes but you could easily gain weight. Build on your communication skills.

2006 Partnerships blossom and you will be happier as part of a team than a solo agent. It is a great year for relationships of all kinds.

2007 Relationships, both professional and personal, continue to flourish. You could receive money through a partner or legacy. Do not neglect your family.

2008 An excellent year to invest in your home and property. Close relationships need your attention and may benefit from major changes.

2009 You feel lucky! Seize the opportunities that come along and be prepared to branch out in new directions. Concentrate on your creative abilities.

2010 A busy year with a lot going on. Focus on your long-term goals and wishes, especially if that involves retraining or learning a new skill.

Cancer   22 June – 22 July

element	**water**
symbol	**crab**
planet	**Moon**
colour	**grey**
gemstone	**pearl**
careers	**childcare, catering, marine biology**
day of the week	**Monday**
area of the body	**chest**

Cancerians are very gentle creatures but they often like to pretend otherwise. Like their namesake crabs, they tend to disguise a very soft centre with a slightly crusty exterior. This is purely for protection because they are so sensitive that they are easily hurt. They also have a tendency to be rather defensive, and assume that someone will be nasty to them even when this is not the case.

A Cancerian's home is their refuge from the world, and they are very choosy about who they allow inside the front door. They lavish a great deal of care and money on their home because it is the centre of their world. When looking for ways to invest money, they should always consider buying property if they can afford it. They also cherish their family, or the people who feel like family to them. Not all Cancerians get on well with their blood relations, but if that is the case they will amass a ready-made family of friends instead.

A Cancerian's emotions are never far from the surface. They need to be loved and take great pleasure in looking after their nearest and dearest. However, they have a tendency to hold on to relationships long after they should have ended, simply because they cannot bear to be left on their own.

the future for Cancer

2001 You need to preserve your privacy and have plenty of time to yourself. Make careful plans for the future. An excellent year to work behind the scenes.

2002 Look out for a fantastic opportunity that cannot be missed. Clever investments pay off but do not overextend yourself financially.

2003 You start to emerge from your shell and are ready to make big changes to your outlook on life. Explore new horizons and be adventurous.

2004 A great year to keep in touch with people who can help you. Your domestic life expands. A new venture goes well, provided you plan it in advance.

2005 Concentrate on your values and priorities in life for maximum happiness. Sober and sensible investments will grow steadily.

2006 A year of great satisfaction. Hard work will bring financial rewards but do not neglect your health. Make invigorating changes to your daily routine.

2007 Communications will go well and it will pay to keep up to date with technology. Matters close to home need careful consideration.

2008 A marvellous year for your relationships although some partnerships need to be re-evaluated. Stay in touch with as many people as possible.

2009 Although some relationships may end, others will begin. Carefully consider ways of boosting your investments and sharing your resources.

2010 A busy year. Keep your options and your mind open to new experiences. Previous hard work brings big rewards, both financially and emotionally.

Leo   23 July – 23 August

element	**fire**
symbol	**lion**
planet	**Sun**
colour	**gold**
gemstone	**ruby**
careers	**entertainment, fashion, sport**
day of the week	**Sunday**
area of the body	**spine**

This is the sign that likes to be in the spotlight. Leos have a great need for applause and recognition, which is why you find so many of them in show business. Even if you know a Leo who will never tread the boards, they will still purr like a cat whenever you praise them. Leos are extremely artistic and creative, and they have an enormous need to express themselves through such talents.

Leos are very organized and are also excellent at organizing others. Sometimes, this means they can be rather bossy and domineering, insisting that they know best. However, most Leos are able to laugh at themselves and apologize when they suspect they have overstepped the mark.

A happy family life is essential for a Leo. They love gathering their nearest and dearest around them, and will take a strong interest in the welfare of all the children they know. Love is another very important part of life for a Leo. Indeed, this is one of the two signs of love, with Libra being the other. This is such an affectionate and demonstrative sign that a Leo will feel stifled and lonely if they do not have anyone to love. They are faithful and loyal, and think that behaving in an untrustworthy or dishonest way is beneath their dignity. They believe, quite rightly, that they are worth more than that.

the future for Leo

2001 Friends are good fun and bring interesting opportunities. Romance blossoms. Your hopes and dreams for the future are closer than you think.

2002 You have good reason to feel optimistic about your future prospects but avoid taking foolish risks. Friends give you solid support and affection.

2003 This is a year to consolidate your financial position rather than expand it. Do not take a close partner for granted or let your relationship stagnate.

2004 Continue to protect your investments and finances when necessary. Relationships bring plenty of surprises but try to go with the flow.

2005 Periods of socializing alternate with the need to be solitary. A great year to extend your home and family life, and also to explore your roots.

2006 Loved ones bring you happiness. Activities that enable you to express yourself give you a fulfilling creative outlet. Look after your health.

2007 A very enjoyable year, especially for love and artistic ventures. Consider changing your job or altering the pattern of your daily routine.

2008 A very good year for hard work and being of service to others. On the whole, it will be wiser to save your money rather than spend it.

2009 Relationships require give and take. It will help to talk things through rather than brood on them by yourself. Work with people rather than against them.

2010 Be adventurous! It is a year for branching out in new directions and also for deciding what you want out of life. Pay attention to your family.

Virgo   24 August – 23 September

element	**earth**
symbol	**maiden**
planet	**Mercury**
colour	**navy blue**
gemstone	**agate**
careers	**secretarial, accountancy, medicine**
day of the week	**Wednesday**
area of the body	**stomach**

Virgos tend to get a bad press because they are always saddled with such epithets as practical, efficient and reliable. It makes them sound like a sensible car, and they hate it. Inside every Virgo is a rebel longing to get out but afraid to show this daring side. Yet even if they keep their inner maverick firmly under wraps they are still great company and good fun. They also have the bonus of being ace communicators, terrific wits and very clever.

If you want something done, always ask a Virgo. They have an innate need to be of service and will always do their best to help out. They are also modest, but although they will deprecate their efforts you will soon realize that you have found someone who is organized, methodical and painstaking. Sometimes, a Virgo can get caught up in details and become too analytical, but this is usually a sign of lurking insecurity. Virgos are very modest and have a surprisingly low opinion of themselves. They are also very critical of their efforts, which they often think are second-rate.

Relationships can be a problem area for Virgos, who find it difficult to handle too much intimacy. They are uncomfortable when they let their guard down, and they feel completely out of their depth when involved in highly charged emotional scenes. They fare better when dealing with situations that require a logical approach.

the future for Virgo

2001 Hard work pays off but do not neglect other areas of your life. You need to cultivate a balance between work and play. Friends are important to you.

2002 The focus is on your career and public reputation. Restore your energy by retreating from the fray every now and then. You need a refuge!

2003 Changes to some relationships leave you wondering where you stand, but things are not as difficult as you imagine. Be positive and strong.

2004 Concentrate on whatever or whoever makes your world go round. Group activities give you the chance to shine and also provide new opportunities.

2005 Your hopes and dreams come one step closer to reality. Short journeys are interesting and introduce you to new contacts. Mix and mingle.

2006 A year for connecting with your roots and doing some nest-building. Do not worry if you are working behind the scenes – your time will come.

2007 After a quiet start it is a great year for your social life. It is also a good opportunity to put personal ventures into action, but take them slowly.

2008 A landmark year in which the focus is on relationships. You really come into your own and your life blossoms, but some associations may end.

2009 Put your talents to good use, both financially and in your work. Look after your health and pay attention to your diet if you want to avoid weight gain.

2010 A hectic year in which events happen quickly. Foster your relationships and consider joining forces with someone. It is not a year to go it alone.

Libra   24 September – 23 October

element	**air**
symbol	**scales**
planet	**Venus**
colour	**pale blue**
gemstone	**sapphire**
careers	**diplomacy, beauty, fashion**
day of the week	**Friday**
area of the body	**kidneys**

This is the sign of balance but it is a myth to say that Librans are always balanced. Instead, they are always striving for balance – a process that can involve wild fluctuations from one extreme to the other. This is one of the reasons they are so famously indecisive, because they can always see another side of the argument. They are also reluctant to commit themselves to a decision in case they unwittingly upset someone in the process. Librans have a horror of appearing rude, inconsiderate or insensitive, and will tie themselves in knots trying to give a favourable impression. However, they can be surprisingly wilful when they really want to get their own way, which is when you discover that Libra is the sign of the iron hand in the velvet glove.

Libra is said to be one of the most attractive signs of the zodiac. Librans are certainly very easy on the eye and they take a lot of trouble with their appearance. Libra is also said to be one of the two signs of love. Librans are never happier than when they love and are loved in return. They have a tendency to fall in love with love and can be very idealistic. They are also reluctant to let partners go because they have a horror of being lonely. Librans need other people to reinforce their own sense of identity, and they feel as though something is missing when they are left on their own for too long.

the future for Libra

2001 Expand the horizons of your life in any way you choose. This is not a year to restrict yourself or limit your options. However, be prudent financially.

2002 You are filled with the spirit of adventure and will love spreading your wings. Concentrate on activities that are educational but enjoyable.

2003 You are in a serious mood and want to make big progress in your career. But be prepared for unexpected changes to your job or daily routine.

2004 It is a year of opportunities, especially in your career and public standing. However, do not neglect the pleasurable side of life.

2005 This is a lucky year, especially if you want to embark on new ventures and turn dreams into reality. Concentrate on friends and group activities.

2006 Continue to focus on your social life and grab the chance to meet more people. It is a good year to get involved in activities in your neighbourhood.

2007 Expand your home and family life. It will be important to feel safe and secure. You will value time on your own but do not neglect your social life.

2008 Pay special attention to your domestic situation. Be prepared to make any necessary changes before they reach crisis point to avoid problems.

2009 You are feeling justifiably optimistic! It is a great year for your love life, but creative ventures also flourish. Grab the chance to express yourself.

2010 Guide personal ventures to a satisfactory conclusion. Keep a close eye on finances, especially if you are considering making solid investments for the future.

Scorpio   24 October – 22 November

element	**water**
symbol	**scorpion**
planet	**Pluto**
colour	**burgundy**
gemstone	**opal**
careers	**research, police, psychotherapy**
day of the week	**Tuesday**
area of the body	**bowels**

Scorpio is the most intense and passionate sign of the zodiac. It is also the most misunderstood sign. This is because it rules all the taboo areas of life and is a blank canvas on which people can project their fears and prejudices. It is true that you will meet the occasional Scorpio who lives up to this sign's reputation for being treacherous, vengeful and power-mad, but most Scorpios are much more moderate than this. They may entertain fantasies about such things, but will often stop themselves from acting them out.

Scorpio is a sign of tremendous endurance and resilience, which may explain why so many Scorpios have very difficult lives. They often experience problems that would defeat other people, yet they somehow manage to take them on the chin. Nevertheless, it can make them wary of getting involved in similar situations again.

Something that Scorpios thoroughly enjoy is intrigue. They love a good mystery, being pretty enigmatic themselves, and often suspect that other people are up to no good. Since they are very private, it can be almost impossible to persuade them to reveal much of themselves. They will end up knowing much more about you than you know about them. In relationships, a Scorpio is loyal and trustworthy, but they can also be plagued by jealousy and possessiveness.

the future for Scorpio

2001 Close relationships flourish this year, but be prepared to let them develop rather than stay as they are. Joint and official finances will go well.

2002 Aim for the top! This is a fantastic year to satisfy an ambition, especially if it will be a challenge. You should also pay attention to your intimate relationships.

2003 Friends and leisure pursuits are good fun and will introduce you to new contacts. Spiritual and educational activities will be beneficial and enjoyable.

2004 You need to balance an adventurous spirit with a need for quiet reflection. Loved ones will act in ways you are not prepared for.

2005 New horizons beckon so be prepared to take a chance. Recent hard work pays off by boosting your reputation, but you will be kept very busy.

2006 You have the chance to make big money but be wary of taking risks. The more effort you make in your career, the greater the rewards.

2007 A busy social life brings light relief from the continued emphasis on your career. Even so, you are riding high so make the most of it!

2008 Plans that seemed mere dreams in the past are now becoming reality, with a little help from you. Expect changes to your immediate neighbourhood.

2009 You start the year in a very sociable mood but gradually develop a need for your own company. Consider working from home or behind the scenes.

2010 A year of many changes. Broaden your domestic horizons. After an enjoyably social phase you become interested in your job prospects.

Sagittarius   23 November – 21 December

element	**fire**
symbol	**archer**
planet	**Jupiter**
colour	**purple**
gemstone	**amber**
careers	**travel, equestrianism, education**
day of the week	**Thursday**
area of the body	**liver**

Sagittarius is the sign of the adventurer and rover. Members of this sign are born with wanderlust in their blood and adore taking off on adventures, whether mentally or physically. A Sagittarian is just as happy when lost in a book as when visiting a new country. They always have a new project on the go. Challenge is something else that appeals to all Sagittarians. They are symbolized by the archer, and they spend their lives shooting metaphorical arrows at far-off targets. They do not always hit these targets but they do their best.

Sagittarians have a very infectious enthusiasm for life, and tend to look on the positive side whenever possible. It is a rare Sagittarian who succumbs to pessimism. Even in the face of apparently insurmountable difficulties, their innate optimism often wins the day.

In emotional relationships, Sagittarians enjoy playing the field. For some of them, the thrill of the chase is much more exciting than coping with a long-term relationship. Some of them prefer to remain single throughout their lives. They have a strong need for emotional freedom and independence, and hate the thought of being tied down by their partner. They need to feel that they are a free agent, even when this is obviously not true and they are happily paired up with someone for life.

the future for Sagittarius

2001 A year to foster your relationships and develop new contacts. Any form of partnership works well now. Joint resources flourish later in the year.

2002 Your social life is enjoyable and introduces you to new contacts. A partnership enters a rocky phase, but will survive if you work hard at it.

2003 Changes to your family and domestic life require an adaptable approach. This is an excellent year to build up your financial position.

2004 Look to the future! Dare you turn a pipe dream into reality? Consolidate your current financial success and consider making further investments.

2005 You are very receptive to spiritual, mystical and philosophical subjects. You may even develop a new belief system or moral code as a result.

2006 Fresh fields beckon yet you are only interested in activities that have meaning and purpose. You are poised on the brink of fantastic opportunities.

2007 Life is offering you terrific scope for personal expansion and big developments in your career. Be realistic when handling your finances.

2008 A very good year financially. You are in a strong position at work and may be given extra responsibility. Try to balance your work with your social life.

2009 Your social life flourishes. A great year for making new contacts and increasing your social circle. You will play an important role within a group or organization.

2010 A hectic year in which you are in great demand socially. Yet you will also value your privacy. Your finances may require a fresh approach.

Capricorn 22 December – 20 January

element	**earth**
symbol	**goat**
planet	**Saturn**
colour	**black**
gemstone	**topaz**
careers	**business, osteopathy, civil service**
day of the week	**Saturday**
area of the body	**skeleton**

Capricorns are hard workers. They have a pronounced sense of responsibility and duty, so it is a rare Capricorn who lets people down or goes back on their word. Such behaviour is usually unthinkable for any self-respecting Capricorn. Earning the respect of other people is essential if a Capricorn is to feel happy and fulfilled. They are very bothered about what other people think of them and will always strive to give a good impression.

In fact, Capricorns are often over-achievers. They are so anxious not to let themselves down that they will work much harder than anyone else and put in extra hours at work. Many of them are workaholics, partly because they enjoy the cut and thrust of their jobs and partly because they are scared that if they ease up on their workload someone else will overtake them. This can cause problems in their relationships, because it can be difficult for them to find the time for a happy home life.

Relationships can also be problematic for Capricorns because they find it difficult to show their feelings. By nature, they are shy and reserved, and they are terrified of making fools of themselves. They therefore tend to let others do the running because they are so scared of being rejected. Nevertheless, when they are in a committed relationship they are faithful, loyal and very protective of their family. You can always count on a Capricorn.

the future for Capricorn

2001 Find a happy medium between work and play. You should also pay attention to your health and find ways to reduce areas of possible stress.

2002 Work keeps you busy but relationships keep you happy. An excellent year to join forces with people, whether for business or pleasure.

2003 Technology starts to play a bigger role in your life. There could be a change to your immediate surroundings. A positive attitude pays off.

2004 A year to make the most of your talents and options. Be adventurous early in the year and then concentrate on boosting your career prospects.

2005 Keep one eye on the future but also take care of the present, especially where your career is concerned. A close relationship needs extra attention.

2006 It is a year for focusing on private matters, such as intimate relationships. Your guardian angel will be busy on your behalf.

2007 You are ready to be in the spotlight once more. Be prepared to push ahead with personal projects and new ventures, especially spiritual ones.

2008 A fabulous year to push back the boundaries of your life and seize opportunities. The more positive your attitude, the better the results.

2009 You start to reap the many rewards from your efforts in 2008. Your finances improve and so does your working reputation. Things are looking good!

2010 A year of many changes and activities. Concentrate on whatever you value in life. Social contacts will introduce you to influential people.

Aquarius 21 January – 18 February

element	**air**
symbol	**water carrier**
planet	**Uranus**
colour	**ultramarine**
gemstone	**aquamarine**
careers	**politics, ecology, technology**
day of the week	**Saturday**
area of the body	**ankles**

Aquarians are very different from the other astrological signs. It is partly their honest and forthright approach, partly their inability to suffer fools gladly and partly their determination to be individuals in their own right. Aquarians have no wish to conform to anyone else's rules, and they can have real problems in dealing with authority. They see no point in respecting authority figures purely because they have reached a powerful position, and if anything are very suspicious of them as a result.

Any Aquarian you meet is unique, and proud of it. Although they have a marvellous capacity for friendship, they are very unsure about the wisdom of belonging to groups because they do not want to be one of the crowd. They are also reluctant to get swept up in the politics and power-plays of big groups.

This is one of the most intelligent signs of the zodiac, and Aquarians are much more interested in people's brains than their bodies. Many of them have a take-it-or-leave-it attitude to sex. Emotional freedom is essential to them, and they will not tolerate possessiveness and jealousy. Even when they are involved in a close relationship, they need time to themselves and they may also enjoy conducting a social life that is independent of their partner. Despite this, they are very supportive of their partner and tremendously loyal to them.

the future for Aquarius

2001 A year of enjoyment and happiness. Your job and health prospects are good, and will be even better if you adopt a positive attitude whenever possible.

2002 You continue to do well at work. This is also a good year to concentrate on your relationships. You will enjoy being part of a team rather than a solo agent.

2003 Relationships continue to flourish, bringing you great happiness. Hard work will pay off but do not let your health suffer. Keep an eye on your finances.

2004 Opportunities are all around you but the trick is to spot them. You are still working hard but may not yet get the recognition you think you deserve.

2005 Your prospects are starting to improve and your efforts at work are appreciated. Relationships need plenty of time and attention.

2006 You get your share of the limelight. After that, focus on your long-term plans and goals. Friendships flourish but a partnership needs some hard work.

2007 Work hard at establishing stronger links with partners and associates. This is also a good year to strengthen your finances and joint resources.

2008 A quiet and reflective year in which to consolidate your relationships. A spiritual quest gives you food for thought and also emotional sustenance.

2009 A busy and lively year in which you are offered many opportunities and prospects for expansion. Educational pursuits are especially successful.

2010 Your life is opening out in many different ways. Be receptive to new ideas and do not limit your options. Your career prospects are fantastic.

Pisces 19 February – 20 March

element	**water**
symbol	**fish**
planet	**Neptune**
colour	**sea green**
gemstone	**amethyst**
careers	**photography, dance, oil industry**
day of the week	**Thursday**
area of the body	**feet**

This is one of the most sensitive signs of the zodiac. Pisceans are remarkably thin-skinned, even if they pretend otherwise. This makes them marvellous at helping other people because they have first-hand knowledge of how tough life can be. Unfortunately, it can also make them very susceptible to slights and hurts, whether intentional or not. They are also very attuned to the atmosphere around them, which means they can absorb difficult energies, much to their detriment.

Pisces is capable of achieving great heights and sinking to tremendous lows. This is therefore the sign of the saint or sinner, mystic or thief, philanderer or devoted partner.

Pisceans live on their emotions. They view life from an emotional standpoint and are therefore very subjective. It is impossible for them to gain any detachment from the situations in which they feel an emotional involvement. Their relationships can be very dramatic because they are lived at such a high emotional pitch. They also find it difficult to make up their minds, and will often agree to do things simply because they do not want to upset everyone. Sometimes, there is a tendency with members of this sign to think of themselves as martyrs. They can certainly be capable of great acts of devotion and self-sacrifice, but there may also be an ego-driven need to be seen as saintly.

the future for Pisces

2001 A marvellous year to lay down roots and establish a happy domestic life. You are inspired in creative pursuits and will get the chance to prove it.

2002 Opportunities come thick and fast, particularly in your career and family life. Consider investing your money in bricks and mortar.

2003 A year to concentrate on your work, health, home and relationships. Be prepared for exciting changes in the direction and pace of your life.

2004 Put your relationships above all else. You will be happier with other people than on your own. Even so, a close alliance goes through a testing time.

2005 You have good reason to feel optimistic. Your finances are looking good and your job prospects are excellent. You will also be given a fantastic challenge.

2006 Spiritual and religious activities bring you many benefits. Your working life continues to prosper, with recognition of your talents and possible promotion.

2007 Keep concentrating on your career. Later in the year, the focus switches to your dreams for the future, which are closer than you think.

2008 Many of the opportunities awaiting you will come through other people, so spend a lot of time cultivating your contacts. Group activities are enjoyable.

2009 A friendship brings advantages. Relationships stir up deep-seated emotions and prompt you to deal with feelings that you have never acknowledged before.

2010 After a quiet start you become increasingly gregarious. Work hard to boost your income, and make the most of your joint resources and investments.

chinese astrology

When Buddha lay dying, he invited all the animals in the world to visit him and pay their last respects. Yet only twelve animals appeared. In gratitude, he offered each one its own year, so that it would be remembered for ever. And thus the Chinese zodiac was born.

This is one of the many legends that explain the Chinese practice of assigning each year to a particular animal, and a particular set of characteristics to all people born within that year. Unfortunately, the truth about the birth of Chinese astrology is likely to be much more prosaic, and ancient Chinese astrology books made no mention of the animal names. Nevertheless,

Chinese astrology is now popular throughout the world, with the Chinese New Year celebrated in the West as well as in the East.

We have the Moon to thank for Chinese astrology. In contrast to Western astrology, which is based on the annual solar cycle (see page 85), Chinese astrology is ruled by the lunar cycle. In Western parlance, the Chinese New Year begins with the New Moon in Aquarius, which always takes place some time between mid-January and mid-February. A lunar year has twelve lunations, a lunation being the length of time from one New Moon to the next. Each lunation lasts twenty-nine and a half days, making a total of 354 days in a lunar year. As this falls short of the solar year, an extra month is added to the lunar calendar roughly every three years, in order to bring the two calendars into line.

This chapter describes the characteristics of the twelve animal signs – Rat, Ox, Tiger, Rabbit, Dragon, Snake, Horse, Goat, Monkey, Rooster, Dog and Pig. If you do not already know your Chinese sign, look through each sign in turn for your year of birth, then check that your date of birth is included within that animal year. If it is not, look at either the previous sign or the next one to find your Chinese sign. Because the Chinese year doesn't start on 1st January, anyone with a birthday in January or early February may find that their Chinese sign is the one before the one they expected.

This chapter also tells you what you can expect to happen in the future, according to the relationship between your Chinese sign and that of the year in question. Each animal year recurs every twelve years, so you can count backwards to discover whether the events of a particular year in your past matched its Chinese forecast.

It is beyond the scope of this book to describe Chinese astrology in more depth. However, if you do choose to investigate it further you will discover that the signs follow a sixty-year cycle in which each animal sign is linked with one of five elements – wood, fire, earth, metal and water. This means there are five variations to each animal sign, so someone born as a Fire Pig will have a slightly different personality from someone born as a Water Pig, although they will both share some Pig characteristics.

Rat

Rat Years

31 January 1900 – 18 February 1901

18 February 1912 – 5 February 1913

5 February 1924 – 23 January 1925

24 January 1936 – 10 February 1937

10 February 1948 – 28 January 1949

28 January 1960 – 14 February 1961

15 February 1972 – 2 February 1973

2 February 1984 – 20 January 1985

19 February 1996 – 6 February 1997

7 February 2008 – 25 January 2009

You cannot help noticing Rats. They are so lively, entertaining and gregarious that it is difficult to ignore them. Besides, they are usually surrounded by a captive audience whom they are holding enthralled with their latest stories. Rats are very voluble creatures who enjoy chatting about whatever happens to be on their mind at the time.

Rats also have a tremendous and infectious sense of humour, and a delightfully light-hearted way of looking at the world. Yet they can be serious when necessary and are especially interested in topics that make them think. They are happily engaged on a life-long quest for knowledge and they see nothing odd in always being engrossed in a particular interest. Such interests can last for years or might end in a couple of weeks, but either way the Rat will be fascinated by it while it lasts. As a result of cramming so much knowledge into their head, a Rat is extremely well informed and is often a good person to ask when you want some advice.

When it comes to relationships, Rats are affectionate and have plenty of friends. They probably have also had more than their fair share of love affairs over the years, and it has to be said that the notion of fidelity is a very foreign concept to some Rats. They never want to be tied down, even when they are.

The future for the Rat

12 Feb 2002 – 31 Jan 2003
Year of the Horse Play safe and do not take unnecessary risks in any area of your life. Be very careful when handling your finances and do not be persuaded to waste your resources.

1 Feb 2003 – 21 Jan 2004
Year of the Goat Your finances are starting to improve. Your plans are making good progress, but be prepared to be flexible and to make any necessary changes. Opportunities abound.

22 Jan 2004 – 8 Feb 2005
Year of the Monkey A good year. Work hard at fostering your relationships, because taking trouble with them now will pay off in the future. You will have good reason to celebrate.

9 Feb 2005 – 28 Jan 2006
Year of the Rooster The celebrations continue! It will be a very busy year, with plenty of exciting and enjoyable events. Balance these hectic periods with lots of rest.

29 Jan 2006 – 17 Feb 2007
Year of the Dog Not an easy year. It will be tempting to allow worries to get on top of you, especially over problems that are out of your hands. Be patient and wait for things to improve.

18 Feb 2007 – 6 Feb 2008
Year of the Pig A year in which to consolidate the progress you have made so far. Be careful when handling your finances. Career moves are largely on hold for the time being.

7 Feb 2008 – 25 Jan 2009
Year of the Rat It's an excellent year for making the most of the opportunities around you. Be as enterprising and adaptable as possible. Financially, it's better to save than to spend.

26 Jan 2009 – 13 Feb 2010
Year of the Ox An enjoyable time in your family life. Other people will be beneficial to you, especially if they are sharing their good fortune. You will have more responsibilities than usual.

14 Feb 2010 – 2 Feb 2011
Year of the Tiger Keep a tight hold of your money and avoid any form of speculation. There could also be confusion to contend with. Travel may be on the cards.

3 Feb 2011 – 22 Jan 2012
Year of the Rabbit You could welcome a new face into the family. Avoid misunderstandings in your close relationships. It is a good year for increasing your business contacts.

23 Jan 2012 – 9 Feb 2013
Year of the Dragon A very happy and successful year, especially in your career and love life. However, watch out for people who want to take advantage of you.

10 Feb 2013 – 30 Jan 2014
Year of the Snake Be prudent and try to save money rather than spend it, in case you encounter some rainy days. Luckily, things will get better as the year progresses.

Ox

Ox Years

19 February 1901	–	7 February 1902
6 February 1913	–	25 January 1914
24 January 1925	–	11 February 1926
11 February 1937	–	30 January 1938
29 January 1949	–	15 February 1950
15 February 1961	–	4 February 1962
3 February 1973	–	22 January 1974
21 January 1985	–	8 February 1986
7 February 1997	–	27 January 1998
26 January 2009	–	13 February 2010

If there were a competition to discover the hardest working member of the Chinese zodiac, the Ox would win hoofs down. They do not understand such concepts as taking life easy, relaxing and not working. Instead, they feel uncomfortable when they are not doing something profitable, industrious or practical – preferably all three.

Oxen are very concerned about protecting their reputation because they always want to be seen in a good light. They dread the idea of being considered unreliable, and if necessary they will work round the clock in order to fulfil an obligation or turn in a good job of work. Their career is a very important part of their life and they will do their utmost to be successful in whatever they set out to achieve. The result can be that they turn into a workaholic who never knows when to down tools and go home. Their family life can suffer, but although their loved ones may complain that they never see their Ox they will not be able to be complain about their standard of living.

When dealing with relationships, Oxen are all at sea. They find it embarrassing to declare their feelings, even though they are capable of deep love. It is simply that they do not want to talk about their emotions for fear of embarrassing themselves or losing face. They need some gentle encouragement first.

The future for the Ox

12 Feb 2002 – 31 Jan 2003
Year of the Horse Not an easy time, although matters will improve later in the year. Take care when handling your financial affairs and your relationships. Do not bite off more than you can chew.

1 Feb 2003 – 21 Jan 2004
Year of the Goat A year in which you feel you are marking time. Nevertheless, you will enjoy some happy and fulfilling relationships. Try not to lose something you value highly.

22 Jan 2004 – 8 Feb 2005
Year of the Monkey
Everything is going well! A wish could be granted or a cherished desire fulfilled. A marvellous time to expand your relationships and your horizons in general.

9 Feb 2005 – 28 Jan 2006
Year of the Rooster An enjoyable year, although certain people are not as trustworthy or reliable as you expect. Overall, you will experience plenty of success and happiness.

29 Jan 2006 – 17 Feb 2007
Year of the Dog Do not panic about problems because they will soon be sorted out. It is not worth worrying about them. A relationship may go through a testing time.

18 Feb 2007 – 6 Feb 2008
Year of the Pig A great year for building up contacts and networks that you can use at a later date. Try not to be fazed by temporary problems with loved ones and colleagues.

7 Feb 2008 – 25 Jan 2009
Year of the Rat You can look forward to a very productive year financially. Clever investments will pay off. You may encounter more responsibilities than usual.

26 Jan 2009 – 13 Feb 2010
Year of the Ox Be patient in the face of minor delays and setbacks. This is a great year for forming new partnerships and alliances, whether for business or pleasure.

14 Feb 2010 – 2 Feb 2011
Year of the Tiger Although you will face a lot of opposition, perseverance will pay off and you will emerge triumphant. Be patient if you do not immediately get the results you expect.

3 Feb 2011 – 22 Jan 2012
Year of the Rabbit Act wisely and carefully in all financial arrangements. Set aside money in case you need it in an emergency. Be selective about who you trust in money and business matters.

23 Jan 2012 – 9 Feb 2013
Year of the Dragon Your plans will see the light of day, but not as quickly as you hope. It is a year when hard work brings rewards. You will also make some excellent contacts.

10 Feb 2013 – 30 Jan 2014
Year of the Snake Life is easy and productive, provided you are flexible and prepared to listen to other people's points of view. If not, you could fall out with someone.

Tiger

Tiger Years

8 February 1902	– 27 January 1903
26 January 1914	– 13 February 1915
12 February 1926	– 1 February 1927
31 January 1938	– 18 February 1939
16 February 1950	– 5 February 1951
5 February 1962	– 24 January 1963
23 January 1974	– 10 February 1975
9 February 1986	– 28 January 1987
28 January 1998	– 15 February 1999
14 February 2010	– 2 February 2011

People born under the Chinese sign of the Tiger share several characteristics with their feline namesakes. For a start, they take a great deal of trouble with their appearance and always want to look as well groomed as possible. They can often be found preening themselves in front of the mirror, checking that they look good. It is highly likely that they are also checking to make sure they do not look like everyone else, because Tigers have a very strong need to stand out from the rest of the crowd.

Tigers are very attracted to fast cars and other ways of getting around quickly. Even if they do not want to run as fast as a tiger in the jungle, they will happily put their car through its paces, trusting that their innate luck will hold and they will not be caught breaking the speed limit.

Tigers have a strong need for emotional independence. Even when involved in a long-standing relationship, they do not want to feel tied down. Yet once they fall in love with someone they will stay with them, even though they may stray every now and then. It is best not to ask questions about any indiscretions that take place. Better simply to enjoy the knowledge that your Tiger is with you because they want to be, not because it is expected of them.

The future for the Tiger

12 Feb 2002 – 31 Jan 2003
Year of the Horse An excellent year! Your home life is happy and fruitful, with good reason to celebrate. Your career prospects are great, with possible promotion and acclaim.

1 Feb 2003 – 21 Jan 2004
Year of the Goat Niggling and petty problems take up a lot of your time. Seize the chance to unwind whenever possible. Nevertheless, you will have much to be thankful for.

22 Jan 2004 – 8 Feb 2005
Year of the Monkey An irritating year, peppered with setbacks and personality clashes. The best way to cope is to strive for co-operation and harmony whenever possible.

9 Feb 2005 – 28 Jan 2006
Year of the Rooster Although you may face what seem like insurmountable problems, they will soon sort themselves out. The trick is not to panic. People will be happy to rally round and help.

29 Jan 2006 – 17 Feb 2007
Year of the Dog A year when hard work pays off. Concentrate on your long-term plans and career goals because they stand an excellent chance of moving forward.

18 Feb 2007 – 6 Feb 2008
Year of the Pig After a very healthy start financially, you need to conserve your resources rather than spend them. Not everyone is as trustworthy as they seem, so be on your guard.

7 Feb 2008 – 25 Jan 2009
Year of the Rat Although this will not be a very exciting year, do not be tempted to spend your way out of boredom. Try to avoid rash and impulsive acts intended to liven things up.

26 Jan 2009 – 13 Feb 2010
Year of the Ox This is not a good year to be rebellious or to invite clashes with authority figures. If you are patient, your problems will soon vanish without the need for conflict.

14 Feb 2010 – 2 Feb 2011
Year of the Tiger You can count on certain people's co-operation and help. Things will go well, but guard against complacency. Be prudent and save your money whenever possible.

3 Feb 2011 – 22 Jan 2012
Year of the Rabbit You will hear some good news, especially in your career and relationships. A year in which you will achieve a great deal and be justifiably proud of yourself.

23 Jan 2012 – 9 Feb 2013
Year of the Dragon You are tempted to hold tight to the status quo, even when it is not in your interests to do so. Avoid being talked into unwise speculation or foolish purchases.

10 Feb 2013 – 30 Jan 2014
Year of the Snake Things will go well, although there could be a few snags in close relationships. Do not become drawn into other people's disputes or problems, as these will cause upsets.

Rabbit

Rabbit Years

28 January 1903	–	15 February 1904
14 February 1915	–	2 February 1916
2 February 1927	–	22 January 1928
19 February 1939	–	7 February 1940
6 February 1951	–	26 January 1952
25 January 1963	–	12 February 1964
11 February 1975	–	30 January 1976
29 January 1987	–	16 February 1988
16 February 1999	–	4 February 2000
3 February 2011	–	22 January 2012

Rabbits need their home comforts. They will soon become unhappy, not to say downright mutinous, if they have to endure sloppy or untidy surroundings for long. It is essential for them to feel comfortable and they will object if they feel they are roughing it or having to endure less than pristine conditions.

Beauty is very dear to any Rabbit's heart. They feel out of sorts and their sensitive nerves become jangled if they are not looking their best. They will spend vast amounts of money on the best clothes and shoes they can possibly afford, and will quickly become upset if their nearest and dearest do not notice the sartorial efforts they have made. If you are going to buy an expensive new outfit and want to take someone along for the benefit of their advice, a Rabbit will give you an honest opinion without hurting your feelings.

Rabbits are born survivors and always seem to emerge from problems smelling of roses. This is probably because they try to think about their troubles as little as possible. A typical Rabbit ignores adversity and pretends that everything is wonderful, because they believe that it could easily turn out that way. If the worst comes to the worst they will deal with it when it happens. Otherwise, they can see no point in ruining their day by fretting.

The future for the Rabbit

**12 Feb 2002 – 31 Jan 2003
Year of the Horse**
Influential people will be very useful to you and may be prepared to pull strings on your behalf. It is a good year for keeping busy with current projects.

**1 Feb 2003 – 21 Jan 2004
Year of the Goat** A year of tremendous success and happiness. Your plans go well and your relationships run smoothly. Money is plentiful but you must attend to complex financial details.

**22 Jan 2004 – 8 Feb 2005
Year of the Monkey** Be positive without being overly optimistic. Although your relationships thrive on the whole, someone is not as trustworthy as you imagined.

**9 Feb 2005 – 28 Jan 2006
Year of the Rooster**
Money is thin on the ground and there are unforeseen expenses. Teamwork will be very helpful in every area of your life. This is not a time to go it alone.

**29 Jan 2006 – 17 Feb 2007
Year of the Dog** Watch out for obstacles in your career. Even so, it will be a happy year in which you accomplish a great deal. Relationships run smoothly and are enjoyable.

**18 Feb 2007 – 6 Feb 2008
Year of the Pig** Try to avoid being too generous and optimistic for your own good. Protect your interests, especially against unexpected events. But it is not all bad by any means.

**7 Feb 2008 – 25 Jan 2009
Year of the Rat** An easy-going year and great for making future plans. However, you will not make quite as much progress as you would like. Even so, you have little to complain about.

**26 Jan 2009 – 13 Feb 2010
Year of the Ox** A tricky year in which you struggle to achieve anything. Do not allow worries or relationship problems to interfere with your health. Changes do not work out.

**14 Feb 2010 – 2 Feb 2011
Year of the Tiger** Be wary about reaching agreements because you may not have all the facts. Try to avoid conflict whenever possible, even if that means being excessively diplomatic.

**3 Feb 2011 – 22 Jan 2012
Year of the Rabbit** A very happy and successful year. Your relationships thrive, your finances blossom and your career goes from strength to strength. There could be unexpected fiscal gains.

**23 Jan 2012 – 9 Feb 2013
Year of the Dragon**
Despite a rather lacklustre time financially, you have plenty to keep you smiling. Your relationships are especially enjoyable, with the chance to make new friends.

**10 Feb 2013 – 30 Jan 2014
Year of the Snake** A year of changes, although you will struggle to make these happen. You may move home, alter your career or be involved in plenty of travelling.

Dragon

Dragon Years

16 February 1904	–	3 February 1905
3 February 1916	–	22 January 1917
23 January 1928	–	9 February 1929
8 February 1940	–	26 January 1941
27 January 1952	–	13 February 1953
13 February 1964	–	1 February 1965
31 January 1976	–	17 February 1977
17 February 1988	–	5 February 1989
5 February 2000	–	23 January 2001
23 January 2012	–	9 February 2013

Here is someone who believes in plain speaking. Dragons in legends breathe fire and anyone born under this sign will have their own way of following that tradition. Every now and then they will utter a hot-headed or inflammatory statement that makes everyone within earshot draw in their breath sharply and wonder what they have done to deserve such an ear-bashing. Yet, unless the Dragon is being deliberately rude or provocative, they cannot understand why their words have such an unfortunate impact on their audience.

Despite their ability to be about as blunt as you can get without provoking physical injury, Dragons are very popular and much loved. This is partly because they are such wonderful examples to the rest of us. They have a remarkable strength of character, immense willpower and redoubtable physical strength. Dragons will not allow themselves to be beaten by any ailments, disabilities or other impediments. They will simply work around them. What is more, they will never draw attention to them.

Although you might approach a sharp-tongued Dragon with trepidation, they are very kind underneath that fiery exterior. They are also deeply troubled to think they may have hurt someone's feelings, because they never mean any harm by it.

The future for the Dragon

12 Feb 2002 – 31 Jan 2003
Year of the Horse
Changes and unforeseen events keep you on your toes. Problems will resolve themselves easily, provided you do not use them as an excuse for disputes and arrogance.

1 Feb 2003 – 21 Jan 2004
Year of the Goat
Not a great year for your career and finances, which are only moderately successful. Yet there is plenty to enjoy in your relationships and domestic life.

22 Jan 2004 – 8 Feb 2005
Year of the Monkey
Things go well, but avoid taking unnecessary risks that might lead to disputes. Strive for compromise and harmony when dealing with partners and loved ones.

9 Feb 2005 – 28 Jan 2006
Year of the Rooster
An excellent year in which to make up for lost time. You may also be able to recoup recent financial losses. Seize the chance to make new friends and other contacts.

29 Jan 2006 – 17 Feb 2007
Year of the Dog
A tense year in which you face unforeseen problems. Try not to get drawn into arguments with people who do not have your best interests at heart.

18 Feb 2007 – 6 Feb 2008
Year of the Pig
Recent difficulties melt away. Relationships are happy and enjoyable. Your career and financial prospects are improving. You will do a lot of travelling.

7 Feb 2008 – 25 Jan 2009
Year of the Rat
An enjoyably busy year in which you have good reason to be pleased with your progress. Relationships flourish and it is especially good for romance.

26 Jan 2009 – 13 Feb 2010
Year of the Ox
You feel as though you are in the eye of the storm as people around you encounter problems, but you remain unscathed. Your family life is very enjoyable.

14 Feb 2010 – 2 Feb 2011
Year of the Tiger
It is hard to make much progress and when you do it involves disputes. You feel stuck in the middle between warring factions. Try not to let worries get on top of you.

3 Feb 2011 – 22 Jan 2012
Year of the Rabbit
A much better year in which you make a lot of progress. Look after your health and general well-being. Your home life is happy and peaceful.

23 Jan 2012 – 9 Feb 2013
Year of the Dragon
A very productive and successful year, with plenty to keep you occupied. It is an especially good time in your career and you will deservedly gain much recognition.

10 Feb 2013 – 30 Jan 2014
Year of the Snake
Another excellent year for business and your career. However, someone will try to oppose you. Do not neglect your relationships; if you do, they will suffer.

Snake

Snake Years

4 February 1905 – 22 January 1906

23 January 1917 – 10 February 1918

10 February 1929 – 29 January 1930

27 January 1941 – 14 February 1942

14 February 1953 – 2 February 1954

2 February 1965 – 21 January 1966

18 February 1977 – 6 February 1978

6 February 1989 – 26 January 1990

24 January 2001 – 11 February 2002

10 February 2013 – 30 January 2014

Whether or not snakes are your favourite reptiles, their equivalent in Chinese astrology is one of the most attractive of the twelve signs. When someone is a Snake, they take great care with their appearance. They also give the impression of being very organized and in command of themselves. Would a Snake ever let you see them ruffled? Never! However, they do need plenty of time to themselves and their nerves will become jangled if they have too much enforced companionship.

Snakes are so cool, graceful and seductive that it's no surprise they are rarely short of admirers. Their stunning good looks help, of course, but they have another, indefinable quality that does wonders for their allure. Perhaps it's the thought that this wonderful person has chosen to be with you when they are obviously in such great demand. Unfortunately, they may remain in great demand, because many Snakes continue to play the field even when they are in a committed relationship. Snakes expect their partners to play by the rules, but may discreetly follow a different set of rules when it suits them.

If you have a knotty problem that you want to discuss with someone, locate your nearest Snake. They are very wise, do not get excited easily, and will give you the benefit of their advice and considerable experience.

The future for the Snake

12 Feb 2002 – 31 Jan 2003 Year of the Horse A marvellous year in which any problems will quickly resolve themselves. Your hopes and dreams will be realized. Brooding on worries could affect your health.

1 Feb 2003 – 21 Jan 2004 Year of the Goat A fantastic year for enjoying your current position. It is a great opportunity to make some good contacts who will turn out to be highly influential and beneficial.

22 Jan 2004 – 8 Feb 2005 Year of the Monkey You will fare best if you keep your head and do not become involved in disputes. You would be wise to stay on the sidelines. People will be helpful when necessary.

9 Feb 2005 – 28 Jan 2006 Year of the Rooster A fabulous year in which you reap the rewards of previous hard work. There could be a big financial improvement, too. Your home life is happy and fulfilling.

29 Jan 2006 – 17 Feb 2007 Year of the Dog Keep an eye open for some great opportunities. You also get the chance to launch new ventures. Travelling is very enjoyable. Look after your health.

18 Feb 2007 – 6 Feb 2008 Year of the Pig Think twice before rushing into anything. Do not allow poor judgement to lead you into rash decisions. Attend to your relationships and sort out any problems sooner rather than later.

7 Feb 2008 – 25 Jan 2009 Year of the Rat A busy year! There is plenty going on, with some great opportunities. It is also a time of growth in your career. Think twice before borrowing or lending money.

26 Jan 2009 – 13 Feb 2010 Year of the Ox Although you will make good progress you will encounter a few obstacles. Try to take things on the chin and reach compromises when necessary.

14 Feb 2010 – 2 Feb 2011 Year of the Tiger Not the easiest of years. Other people are difficult to cope with and will test your patience. Do not become drawn into needless disputes or try to get your own back.

3 Feb 2011 – 22 Jan 2012 Year of the Rabbit You have plenty to keep you busy, and leisure time will be at a premium. You stand to gain a lot of money, but you might spend a great deal of it as well!

23 Jan 2012 – 9 Feb 2013 Year of the Dragon After a difficult start in which you have to contend with difficult people, life becomes much easier. Avoid unnecessary extravagance and try to save rather than spend.

10 Feb 2013 – 30 Jan 2014 Year of the Snake A year for maintaining your current position rather than trying to expand. This may feel frustrating so do not do anything rash because you feel impatient.

Horse

Horse Years

23 January 1906	– 11 February 1907
11 February 1918	– 31 January 1919
30 January 1930	– 16 February 1931
15 February 1942	– 4 February 1943
3 February 1954	– 23 January 1955
22 January 1966	– 8 February 1967
7 February 1978	– 27 January 1979
27 January 1990	– 14 February 1991
12 February 2002	– 31 January 2003
31 January 2014	– 18 February 2015

Life is never dull when a Horse is around. Members of this sign are in love with life and want to extract as much enjoyment out of it as possible. Even when a Horse is in their eighties and beyond, they will still be busy exploring new ideas and developing exciting projects while their non-Horse contemporaries are allowing their mental and physical horizons to shrink. As far as a Horse is concerned, you should get as much zest out of every day as possible.

The last thing a Horse enjoys is enforced idleness. They soon become fidgety and restless, and they can even make themselves ill if their life becomes too sedentary or predictable. They like to do things on the spur of the moment because it makes life so interesting. Besides, they are reluctant to plan too far in advance in case they change their mind about what they want to do.

This is a very intelligent, erudite and quick-witted sign. A Horse is nobody's fool. They are also extremely creative and practical, so they enjoy activities that involve using their hands, such as painting, sewing and pottery. Tasks that they consider to be sheer drudgery, such as cleaning, leave them cold and, if they can afford it, they will pay someone else to take care of that side of life. The Horse is too busy having fun to want to pick up a duster!

The future for the Horse

**12 Feb 2002 – 31 Jan 2003
Year of the Horse** A marvellous year, especially where money is concerned. Things go well with little effort from you. Be prepared to rebuild a tricky relationship.

**1 Feb 2003 – 21 Jan 2004
Year of the Goat** A house move or long-distance travel is likely. It is a very enjoyable year in which everything runs smoothly and you have good reason to feel optimistic.

**22 Jan 2004 – 8 Feb 2005
Year of the Monkey** A year of surprises. Unexpected gains give you a tremendous boost. You will achieve your objectives, but should be prepared for some unforeseen incidents.

**9 Feb 2005 – 28 Jan 2006
Year of the Rooster** You enjoy a happy home life, but may be worried about your career. Try not to let setbacks assume massive proportions, because they can be overcome more easily than you fear.

**29 Jan 2006 – 17 Feb 2007
Year of the Dog** A terrific year for putting your brain to good use. You will enjoy stretching yourself mentally and will be noticed by people in power and authority.

**18 Feb 2007 – 6 Feb 2008
Year of the Pig** There will be frustration due to obstacles and delays beyond your control. You may also experience some financial hitches. Things improve in the second half of the year.

**7 Feb 2008 – 25 Jan 2009
Year of the Rat** Not an easy year, especially in your relationships. Be prudent when making financial decisions and think twice before lending or borrowing money or possessions.

**26 Jan 2009 – 13 Feb 2010
Year of the Ox** A year when hard work will enable you to achieve your goals. Try to have as much control over your life as possible. You will make some financial gains.

**14 Feb 2010 – 2 Feb 2011
Year of the Tiger** A busy and enjoyable year, but it could be expensive! It is a great chance to add to your store of knowledge, whether for business or pleasure.

**3 Feb 2011 – 22 Jan 2012
Year of the Rabbit** An especially good year for your finances and travel. Relationships will keep you happy but fully occupied. There is good news about the family.

**23 Jan 2012 – 9 Feb 2013
Year of the Dragon** A year of ups and downs. Try not to allow worries to prey on your nerves or make you despondent because things are not nearly as bad as they may seem.

**10 Feb 2013 – 30 Jan 2014
Year of the Snake** You feel as though you are taking one step forwards and two steps back. It will be difficult to make much progress, despite your best efforts. Your family life is happy.

Goat

Goat Years

12 February 1907	–	1 February 1908
1 February 1919	–	19 February 1920
17 February 1931	–	6 February 1932
5 February 1943	–	24 January 1944
24 January 1955	–	11 February 1956
9 February 1967	–	28 January 1968
28 January 1979	–	15 February 1980
15 February 1991	–	3 February 1992
1 February 2003	–	21 January 2004
19 February 2015	–	8 February 2016

If there are any Goats in your life, do your best to look after them. They are very tender-hearted, sensitive and vulnerable creatures, even if they do not always give that impression. You may even accidentally hurt their feelings if you take them for granted, assume they are more robust than they really are or appear to reject them.

If a Goat is to feel happy and fulfilled, they need someone or something to love. And preferably both! For example, they might dote on some cherished pets as well as close family and friends. Although Goats adore the idea of being part of a happy family, they do not always experience it for themselves. When this happens, they will create their own family from treasured friends.

Goats are notoriously capricious, so do not expect the Goats of your acquaintance to do what is expected of them. They are a law unto themselves and, sometimes, you may even seriously doubt their sanity when they do things that take you by complete surprise or seem to fly in the face of reason. Goats are also profoundly creative and enjoy experimenting with their artistic abilities, often with mixed results. Yet this is all part of their charm: you never know what they are going to do next and it is great fun discovering what their next adventure will be.

The future for the Goat

12 Feb 2002 – 31 Jan 2003
Year of the Horse
Something that has been a problem in the past has beneficial consequences. Things run smoothly and obstacles are easily overcome. Your health is good.

1 Feb 2003 – 21 Jan 2004
Year of the Goat After an encouraging and sociable start, the year becomes more difficult. You may face financial problems or other restrictions on your time and energy.

22 Jan 2004 – 8 Feb 2005
Year of the Monkey A lively and satisfying year in which everything goes well. You are especially successful in your career and can look forward to well-deserved gains.

9 Feb 2005 – 28 Jan 2006
Year of the Rooster You will have a great time, but will spend a lot of money in the process. Try not to end up out of pocket. You will have to find a balance between compromise and confrontation.

29 Jan 2006 – 17 Feb 2007
Year of the Dog A difficult year in which you face challenges and obstacles. Do your best to remain positive but prudent. Consolidate your position rather than trying to expand it.

18 Feb 2007 – 6 Feb 2008
Year of the Pig Your prospects start to improve, but you are on your guard. Pay attention to your home life. You are wary of others, but should be careful not become overly suspicious of them.

7 Feb 2008 – 25 Jan 2009
Year of the Rat A marvellous year in which you gain many financial benefits, some of them unexpected. Business and career matters look good, as do your relationships.

26 Jan 2009 – 13 Feb 2010
Year of the Ox Personality clashes and misunderstandings need careful attention. It will be better to save money rather than spend it, as this is not a good year financially.

14 Feb 2010 – 2 Feb 2011
Year of the Tiger A varied year. Stay on your toes when dealing with competitors. Nevertheless, you will make some very favourable contacts through work. Your domestic life blossoms.

3 Feb 2011 – 22 Jan 2012
Year of the Rabbit A happy and successful year, especially in your finances and long-term plans. Be prepared for minor skirmishes at home. Avoid making foolhardy decisions.

23 Jan 2012 – 9 Feb 2013
Year of the Dragon
Although you will not make as much progress as you would like, things will go well on the whole. Be prudent when dealing with your finances and do not take risks.

10 Feb 2013 – 30 Jan 2014
Year of the Snake Travel is beneficial and relationships introduce you to new contacts. Despite temporary setbacks and discouraging news, you will make a great deal of progress.

Monkey

Monkey Years

2 February 1908	–	21 January 1909
20 February 1920	–	7 February 1921
7 February 1932	–	25 January 1933
25 January 1944	–	12 February 1945
12 February 1956	–	30 January 1957
29 January 1968	–	16 February 1969
16 February 1980	–	4 February 1981
4 February 1992	–	22 January 1993
22 January 2004	–	8 February 2005
9 February 2016	–	27 January 2017

Life is never dull when a Monkey is around. They are such gifted raconteurs that they can be guaranteed to keep you entertained with tales of their latest exploits. Everyone should know at least a couple of Monkeys, because they are such terrific company and so funny. However, you must be prepared for them to bend the truth a little if that will make what they are saying funnier or more effective. Monkeys can have a flimsy grasp of the facts and will sometimes turn a blind eye to strict detail because it interferes with the pace of their story. Most Monkeys leave it at that, but occasionally you will encounter one who is downright dishonest.

If a Monkey is to be happy, their life must be full of drama. Whenever life threatens to become boring, Monkeys will liven things up in their inimitable way, by developing a new project or venture into which they can channel all their energy, especially if it looks like a hopeless task to everyone else. Yet the Monkey will emerge triumphant, ready for the next challenge.

Monkeys are very popular, but it is a rare member of this sign who has not fallen out with a few friends and loved ones at some point. They usually kiss and make up in the end, though – most of us miss our Monkey friends too much to be estranged from them for long.

The future for the Monkey

12 Feb 2002 – 31 Jan 2003
Year of the Horse You may have to lower your sights if you want to achieve your goals. Keep on your toes for the best results. Try not to let worries and difficulties prey on your mind.

1 Feb 2003 – 21 Jan 2004
Year of the Goat Money comes in easily but it goes out again in the same fashion. Be selective about whom you confide in. You will make some influential contacts.

22 Jan 2004 – 8 Feb 2005
Year of the Monkey A terrific year for taking the initiative and beginning new projects. Entrepreneurial ventures go well. However, do not push yourself to the limit.

9 Feb 2005 – 28 Jan 2006
Year of the Rooster You are in a good position for proceeding with your plans. Try not to let your relationships and health suffer by taking on too much work or too many commitments.

29 Jan 2006 – 17 Feb 2007
Year of the Dog Not an easy year as some plans will not work out, yet you will learn a great deal through the benefit of hindsight. Be careful when handling your finances.

18 Feb 2007 – 6 Feb 2008
Year of the Pig Do not be too trusting because people could be duplicitous. It is best to work by yourself now. The problems you face will be resolved through compromise.

7 Feb 2008 – 25 Jan 2009
Year of the Rat A fortunate year, bringing unexpected gains. This is a marvellous time for speculation, provided it is thought through carefully. Your family life expands.

26 Jan 2009 – 13 Feb 2010
Year of the Ox You do not make as much progress as you would like. There could also be some financial losses. This is not a year for over-expansion or over-ambition.

14 Feb 2010 – 2 Feb 2011
Year of the Tiger A difficult year in which you feel vulnerable, and taken advantage of as a result. Consolidate your current position rather than trying to expand it in any way.

3 Feb 2011 – 22 Jan 2012
Year of the Rabbit You have good reason to feel optimistic about your prospects. Your life is flourishing and this is an excellent year to embark on new ventures and fresh opportunities.

23 Jan 2012 – 9 Feb 2013
Year of the Dragon A fabulous year for expanding your knowledge and increasing your expertise. However, do not expect instant results. Be cautious and conservative in your finances.

10 Feb 2013 – 30 Jan 2014
Year of the Snake Despite some domestic problems, this is a good year. Friends are helpful and you make progress in your career. However, conflicts and disputes will backfire on you badly.

Rooster

Rooster Years

22 January 1909	–	9 February 1910
8 February 1921	–	27 January 1922
26 January 1933	–	13 February 1934
13 February 1945	–	1 February 1946
31 January 1957	–	18 February 1958
17 February 1969	–	5 February 1970
5 February 1981	–	24 January 1982
23 January 1993	–	9 February 1994
9 February 2005	–	28 January 2006
28 January 2017	–	15 February 2018

The Rooster brand of honesty can take some getting used to. Roosters don't like to mince words – they simply don't have the time. This means they have a rather unfortunate knack of accidentally putting both feet in it. Over the years, a Rooster amasses a tremendous range of knowledge which they file away neatly in their brain. When they hear something that rings a bell, their computer-like mind spits out the relevant pieces of information, but not necessarily in the right order. Hence the uncomfortable silence that often follows some Rooster advice. Yet the nub of it is usually completely sound.

One clue to the Rooster character is to think about the role that roosters play in farmyards. It's the rooster who greets each day with his cockcrow, waking up the rest of the flock and probably half the neighbourhood too. A Rooster likes to be first with the news, and what they say may wake everyone up because it's so clever or radical. A Rooster thoroughly enjoys devising schemes and projects, and they've usually got at least one on the go. They can get involved in ideas that are too complex for anyone else. Yet the Rooster will somehow manage to keep everything ticking over. If the project doesn't work out, Roosters will accept defeat with stoic resignation, do their best to learn from their mistakes, and then embark on the next project. They have an indomitable spirit.

The future for the Rooster

12 Feb 2002 – 31 Jan 2003
Year of the Horse You are confronted by many obstacles, but you will surmount them provided you are not over-optimistic. Be prepared to reach compromises in your career.

1 Feb 2003 – 21 Jan 2004
Year of the Goat An enjoyable year in which you make up for any recent lack of progress. Your career and long-term goals look good. It is a time to relax and enjoy life.

22 Jan 2004 – 8 Feb 2005
Year of the Monkey
Proceed with caution, especially if you face money worries, difficult relationships or career problems. Do not automatically believe what others tell you.

9 Feb 2005 – 28 Jan 2006
Year of the Rooster A good year. Recent problems are easily solved, although you must still be careful when handling partners. You gain support from people with influence and authority.

29 Jan 2006 – 17 Feb 2007
Year of the Dog An enjoyable and lively year that is particularly good for travel. It is easy to make things happen. However, you may be haunted by a secret worry or regret.

18 Feb 2007 – 6 Feb 2008
Year of the Pig A year when anything can and will happen, so plan accordingly. Do not take risks and be careful when handling your finances. Someone could give you misleading advice.

7 Feb 2008 – 25 Jan 2009
Year of the Rat Not an easy year, either financially or emotionally. You need to take a moderate approach and to work through your problems by yourself.

26 Jan 2009 – 13 Feb 2010
Year of the Ox Your prospects start to improve and you receive outside support. Travel is enjoyable and your home life is happy. Look after your health.

14 Feb 2010 – 2 Feb 2011
Year of the Tiger A profitable and busy year. Your finances improve as a result of good career moves. Events take place quickly. You have good reason to feel optimistic but do not be foolhardy.

3 Feb 2011 – 22 Jan 2012
Year of the Rabbit A conservative approach pays off. Keep a close eye on your finances and avoid risky speculation. Teamwork will be more productive than being a solo agent.

23 Jan 2012 – 9 Feb 2013
Year of the Dragon A marvellously successful and prosperous year. You gain a lot of power and more control over your own future. Do not allow setbacks to affect your health.

10 Feb 2013 – 30 Jan 2014
Year of the Snake You are able to maintain your current position and make progress. Be prudent when handling your finances and avoid risky speculation or rash moves.

Dog

Dog Years

10 February 1910	–	29 January 1911
28 January 1922	–	15 February 1923
14 February 1934	–	3 February 1935
2 February 1946	–	21 January 1947
19 February 1958	–	7 February 1959
6 February 1970	–	26 January 1971
25 January 1982	–	12 February 1983
10 February 1994	–	30 January 1995
29 January 2006	–	17 February 2007
16 February 2018	–	4 February 2019

Ultra dependable and faithful, Dogs definitely have their hearts in the right place. These are the people who would gladly give you their last square of chocolate if you wanted it. They are tireless fighters against injustice and supporters of good causes because they need life to be as balanced as possible. A Dog is the sort of person who cannot be truly happy if their neighbour is miserable: someone else's suffering will always put a crimp in their day.

Although Dogs are so good at championing other people's causes, they are not so hot at looking after their own interests. Their trusting natures mean they often lay themselves wide open to deception and trickery. Anyone else would have seen it coming, but a Dog is always caught unawares.

Although Dogs are faithful, affectionate and kind, just like man's best friend, they also have the canine trait of biting. In the case of a human Dog, it is their words that bite. They do not intend to offend or be critical, but sometimes they will make a comment that leaves everyone reeling with shock and disbelief. The Dog will also be stunned that they could have said such a thing. They may even lose sleep over it. They are too sensitive and considerate not to feel wretched when they accidentally hurt someone.

The future for the Dog

12 Feb 2002 – 31 Jan 2003 Year of the Horse A fabulous year, full of success and satisfaction. Your career goes well and your finances improve. You are riding high. There will be plenty of travel.

1 Feb 2003 – 21 Jan 2004 Year of the Goat It pays to be patient now because conflict will lead to relationship problems. This is a year for biding your time. Try not to let worries get you down.

22 Jan 2004 – 8 Feb 2005 Year of the Monkey A busy year, although not as successful as you would like. Even so, you will enjoy a hectic social life, with plenty of travel. There could be a house move.

9 Feb 2005 – 28 Jan 2006 Year of the Rooster A difficult year in which your fortunes take a temporary dip. Do not overextend yourself financially. Friends are sometimes hard to understand.

29 Jan 2006 – 17 Feb 2007 Year of the Dog A quiet but enjoyable year. You will make some gains in your career and you could consider increasing your skills. It is certainly a good year for education.

18 Feb 2007 – 6 Feb 2008 Year of the Pig Friends play a big role in your life and you enjoy expanding your social circle. Speculation and investments go well, but fail to live up to your high expectations.

7 Feb 2008 – 25 Jan 2009 Year of the Rat A terrific year, particularly where business and finances are concerned. You enjoy good health. There could be possible problems with your home or family.

26 Jan 2009 – 13 Feb 2010 Year of the Ox It is difficult to know where you stand. Do not reach hasty conclusions, especially if you start to panic. Partners need careful handling and plenty of tact.

14 Feb 2010 – 2 Feb 2011 Year of the Tiger An enjoyable year – you will be in great demand with loved ones. Problems in relationships will be fleeting and easily resolved. Everything is going well!

3 Feb 2011 – 22 Jan 2012 Year of the Rabbit A great chance to focus on your goals and career because you can make huge progress. It is an ideal time to launch a new business venture or pool your resources with a partner.

23 Jan 2012 – 9 Feb 2013 Year of the Dragon A time of hard work, in which you struggle to maintain your current position. You feel as though the odds are stacked against you. It is better to work with others than by yourself.

10 Feb 2013 – 30 Jan 2014 Year of the Snake Your efforts pay off, bringing you acclaim and success. Business dealings go well and you benefit from sound advice. Relax and take life easy – you have earned it.

Pig

Pig Years

30 January 1911	**–**	**17 February 1912**
16 February 1923	**–**	**4 February 1924**
4 February 1935	**–**	**23 January 1936**
22 January 1947	**–**	**9 February 1948**
8 February 1959	**–**	**27 January 1960**
27 January 1971	**–**	**14 February 1972**
13 February 1983	**–**	**1 February 1984**
31 January 1995	**–**	**18 February 1996**
18 February 2007	**–**	**6 February 2008**
23 January 2012	**–**	**9 February 2013**

Pigs are so good-hearted and kind that you can sometimes wonder whether they are genuine. Yet they have no ulterior motives for being so considerate, doing you favours or generally bending over backwards to help out in times of trouble. It is simply the way they are made, and we all have good reason to be thankful for it. Pigs are usually unaware that they have done anything special for you, which only adds to their charm. It also makes it even more important to show your appreciation for them.

Pigs are among the most loving members of the Chinese zodiac. Affectionate and friendly, they are deservedly popular and have a legion of devoted fans. Unfortunately, however, they are sometimes easy prey for people who try to take advantage of them. They often fail to learn from their mistakes, too, so may find themselves at the mercy of a succession of people because they are too kind-hearted to refuse their requests.

Temptation plays a large role in a Pig's life. They have an on-going love affair with food, drink and anything else that brings them comfort and conviviality. They are also strongly tempted to avoid facing unpleasant facts, which can lead to problems when reality finally catches up with them. Ideally, they need loved ones who will help them to deal with the trickier side of life.

The future for the Pig

12 Feb 2002 – 31 Jan 2003
Year of the Horse It is important to be prudent with your finances and selective about whom you trust. Benefits that you did not receive in the past are now forthcoming.

1 Feb 2003 – 21 Jan 2004
Year of the Goat Not a brilliant year for your finances, but you will gain a great deal from other areas of your life. Focus on boosting your career prospects and planning for the future.

22 Jan 2004 – 8 Feb 2005
Year of the Monkey You will not have as much money or backing as you would like. Yet any problems you experience will be minimal and easily solved, especially with the help of others.

9 Feb 2005 – 28 Jan 2006
Year of the Rooster A year of gains and losses. Your career hits setbacks, but you enjoy a very happy domestic life. Channel a lot of effort into overcoming hurdles and reaching compromises.

29 Jan 2006 – 17 Feb 2007
Year of the Dog Do not set your sights too high or you will be disappointed. Do not spread yourself too thinly. Problems from the past could come back to haunt you.

18 Feb 2007 – 6 Feb 2008
Year of the Pig Your prospects improve and you make good progress. Do not take your health and general well-being for granted. Your life is enhanced by new friends and fresh opportunities.

7 Feb 2008 – 25 Jan 2009
Year of the Rat An uncertain year, with your home life and career going through an unsettled phase. Worries will weigh you down, yet you will overcome your difficulties.

26 Jan 2009 – 13 Feb 2010
Year of the Ox A marvellous year for branching out on your own in your career or making the best use of your talents and abilities. Your relationships are complicated.

14 Feb 2010 – 2 Feb 2011
Year of the Tiger Not an easy year. Be conservative with your money and try to set aside something for a rainy day. It may be better to do things yourself rather than to place your trust in others.

3 Feb 2011 – 22 Jan 2012
Year of the Rabbit A good year in which you make modest progress. Your finances are looking healthy and you make some sound decisions. Your home life is happy and satisfying.

23 Jan 2012 – 9 Feb 2013
Year of the Dragon A great time to impress authority figures and co-operate with colleagues. You could find yourself in an influential position. Take care of your health.

10 Feb 2013 – 30 Jan 2014
Year of the Snake A busy year in which things go well. Close relationships need careful handling and much understanding. Do not be extravagant with your money.

the oracle

Centuries ago, an oracle was a special place where people consulted the gods, usually through a priestess. The ancient Greeks were renowned for their use of oracles, one of the most famous being the Pythian oracle at Delphi. Here, a woman known as the Pythia would fall into a trance, during which she would utter pronouncements believed to come directly from the god Apollo. Priests would then interpret what she said.

This form of divination was very much of its time. The gods in classical Greece, when they were not living on Mount Olympus, were believed to move in disguise among ordinary mortals, and poor weather, rough seas, bad harvests and other natural events were blamed on their capricious moods. It was therefore essential to approach the gods in the correct manner to avoid arousing their wrath, which could have swift and disastrous consequences. Artemis, for instance, thought nothing of striking Actaeon blind for having the temerity to look at her while she was bathing.

One way to talk to the gods was through the oracles, which gave the ancient Greeks a direct line to a deity. Today, it is widely believed that the oracles' responses were neither precise nor easily intelligible. They required careful thought, and possibly even some intuition, on the part of the seeker to interpret the often ambiguous message they had been given.

The oracles in this chapter may not come directly from the Greek gods but they do share astrological affinities with them. Each oracle is linked to one of the ten planets of the astrological pantheon and answers questions associated with the areas of life ruled by that planet. For example, since the planet Venus describes how we relate to others, the Venus oracle in this chapter answers questions about relationships. It is heart-shaped to emphasize this. Jupiter rules abundance, so the Jupiter oracle is shaped like a cornucopia – one of the objects traditionally associated with this planet.

when and how to use the oracles

Oracles are especially useful when you need an immediate answer to a question, or when you want to seek guidance about a particular area of your life. As with the other techniques in this book, the oracle will work most effectively when you approach it with respect. If you regard it as little more than a party trick, it will respond accordingly. It may even give you nonsensical answers.

Look through the following pages to see which planetary oracle will best answer your question. Within its shape, you will see nine numbers. Each number refers to a particular answer that appears on that page. Place the book in front of you, concentrate on your question and rotate the book three times in a clockwise direction. Then, still keeping the question in your mind, point your index finger, close your eyes and put your finger on the page. Open your eyes to see where your finger has landed within the shape. If it lands directly on a number, consult that number in the list of answers for the oracle's message. If your finger has landed between two numbers, you can either see which one is nearest and take that as your answer, or you can try again. If, after several attempts, your finger has still not landed on a number, you may decide that the oracle does not wish to speak to you at the moment, and that you would do better to try again another day. When this happens, you may find that the question resolves itself in the meantime so there is no need to ask it again.

the rays of the Sun

In astrology, the Sun represents our creativity and the qualities that make each one of us an individual. This is the oracle to consult when you are looking for new ways to express yourself, or when you have encountered problems with an artistic project.

1 Be flexible and prepared to alter your plans.
2 Everything is going well and success is assured.
3 Do not underestimate your abilities.
4 Someone is ready to help you.
5 False modesty is holding you back.
6 It is time to try something new.
7 Do not be afraid to be different.
8 Keep up the hard work.
9 The answers lie deep within you.

the chalice of the Moon

The Moon rules our instincts and emotions. We speak of 'containing' our emotions, which is why a chalice has been chosen to represent the Moon here. Consult this oracle when you want to understand your innermost thoughts and instinctive reactions.

1 Fear is at the root of your current reactions.
2 You need reassurance from a loved one.
3 Think very carefully about your hidden motives.
4 Do not fall into the trap of being vengeful.
5 You are feeling restless and edgy.
6 Keep control of your temper.
7 Avoid being overly defensive.
8 Work hard at understanding yourself.
9 You need to protect yourself.

the letter of Mercury

Mercury rules our communication skills: the way we think and talk, and our ability to get on with others. This is the oracle to consult when you are facing communication problems.

I   You are not being as straightforward as you imagine.
2   Be prepared to speak from your heart.
3   It is time to write an important letter.
4   Someone should not be trusted.
5   Be honest without being hurtful.
6   You are at cross-purposes with someone.
7   Compromise is necessary.
8   It is essential to say what you think.
9   Do not let wishful thinking blur the facts.

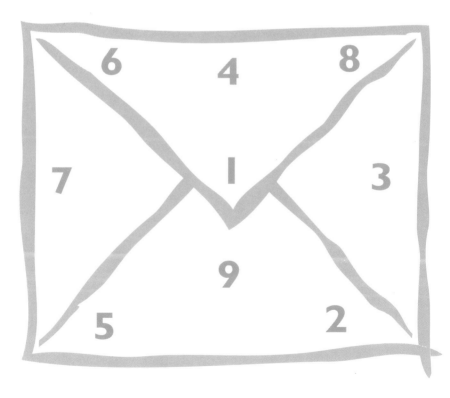

the heart of Venus

Since Venus is the planet of love and romance, the heart is a classic symbol for this oracle. Consult it when you need insight into your relationships.

1 A new love is poised to enter your life.

2 Possessiveness will not win you your heart's desire.

3 A problematic situation will soon resolve itself.

4 A stubborn attitude threatens to come between you and a lover.

5 What begins as a harmless flirtation could become too hot to handle.

6 A cherished wish will soon come true.

7 Someone finds you very attractive.

8 Someone from the past will soon contact you.

9 You are playing with fire.

the rocket of Mars

Mars rules our ambition, drive and energy. The rocket symbolizes the power, thrust and speed of Mars. This is the oracle to consult when you want to know where you are heading in life.

1 Channel your energy in a new direction.
2 Avoid being overly aggressive.
3 Keep on keeping on.
4 Do not waste your time on a wild goose chase.
5 Find a constructive outlet for your energy.
6 Someone is being ruthlessly ambitious.
7 Do not be selfish.
8 Your current project is worth pursuing.
9 Do not lose sight of the end result.

the cornucopia of Jupiter

Abundance and prosperity are ruled by Jupiter, the planet of large amounts of money. The cornucopia is traditionally associated with Jupiter. Use this oracle when you need guidance about your financial position and your values in life.

1 Overspending could soon become an expensive habit.
2 A windfall is coming your way.
3 Chase up money that is owed to you.
4 Your talents are worth more than you realize.
5 Something that seems like a good bet contains hidden snags.
6 An investment of your time or money will be very profitable.
7 There is more to life than financial prosperity.
8 A friend will bring you wonderful opportunities.
9 There are great riches in the smallest areas of life.

the hourglass of Saturn

Saturn rules time, hard work and patience, all of which we need when trying to build a successful career. The hourglass is a classic Saturnian symbol. Consult this oracle when you want guidance about your career.

1   You are working too hard.
2   Avoid shouldering other people's responsibilities.
3   You will soon attain a goal.
4   Your talents are not being recognized.
5   Consider changing your job.
6   A great opportunity is within your grasp.
7   Do not spread yourself too thin.
8   You are making tremendous progress.
9   Have more faith in yourself.

the conundrum of Uranus

Uranus brings shocks and surprises, so a question mark is an apt symbol for this perplexing planet. Consult this oracle when you are confronted by an unexpected event, and want some guidance as to what it means.

I   The surprises are not over yet.
2   What can you learn from this situation?
3   Someone will pull the rug out from under you.
4   The outcome will be better than you expected.
5   Do not underestimate your resilience.
6   Await further developments before making a decision.
7   All you can do is go with the flow.
8   Do not cling to the status quo.
9   You need to be more flexible.

the cloud of Neptune

Neptune is the planet of dreams and fantasies, represented by this cloud. Consult this oracle when you want to know whether a dream will materialize.

1 You are confusing fact and fantasy.
2 Today's dream will become tomorrow's reality.
3 You want something that is unattainable.
4 Someone is stringing you along.
5 Do not promise more than you can deliver.
6 Remain focused on your primary goal.
7 You are fooling yourself.
8 Do not confuse intuition with wishful thinking.
9 A cherished wish will come true.

the volcano of Pluto

Pluto governs major change, which often feels like an earthquake
or volcano when it takes place. Consult this oracle when you are
in the grip of huge changes or are wondering whether you
should initiate them.

1 You cannot not control this situation.
2 You must accept the circumstances beyond your control.
3 You are in a process of tremendous transformation.
4 Keep a firm grip on your emotions.
5 Surrender to a greater power.
6 You have reached a turning point; use it wisely.
7 You are not as powerless as you feel.
8 You must bow to the inevitable.
9 You can still salvage this situation.

runes

Casting runes is one of the most mysterious divination techniques known to man. Steeped in the vivid, often bloodthirsty myths of Viking history, runes still carry the fragmented memories of another world. Legend says that, in order to learn about life and death, the Norse god Odin impaled himself with a spear and hung upside down from Yggdrasil, the Tree of the World. After nine days and nights without water or food, he achieved enlightenment and saw the runes lying beneath him. This is where the rune story starts. Later, priests of Odin used them to tell fortunes. Although they are now often perceived as a so-called New Age technique, runes are actually centuries old.

Yet runes are more than a divination technique. They are also an alphabet, and in ancient times it was believed that they offered protection against evil when carved on tombstones. Today, many people translate their names into the runic alphabet for extra luck or power. Such a name is known as a 'sigil'. A rune can also be carried as a talisman or used as a meditation tool if you want to understand its meaning on a deep level. It can even be used for healing.

Runes have existed in several forms over the centuries. The one most commonly used today consists of twenty-four runes and is known as the Elder Futhark, after the first six runes whose initial letters together spell 'futhark'. The Elder Futhark is divided into three 'aetts' or families of eight runes, each ruled by a particular god. The first set is Freyja's aett, which represents growth. The second is Haegl's aett, representing the elements, and the third is Tyr's aett, symbolizing courage. Some rune sets also include a blank, sometimes called 'wyrd', which is separate from the three aetts. It is used when casting the runes but not in other runic practices. It represents karma and indicates a turning point in the questioner's life. However, the blank rune is not used by traditional runemasters who say it is a bogus modern invention. As you become more comfortable with runes, you may decide to work with it or choose to ignore it.

Runes carry tremendous power, partly because centuries of use have invested them with great meaning and resonance. When casting the runes, it is helpful to remember that these symbols or glyphs have not changed for hundreds of years. They are especially informative when you want to gain an overview of a situation. They often speak in symbolic language which can be difficult at first, but once you become attuned to runes you will marvel at their accuracy and power.

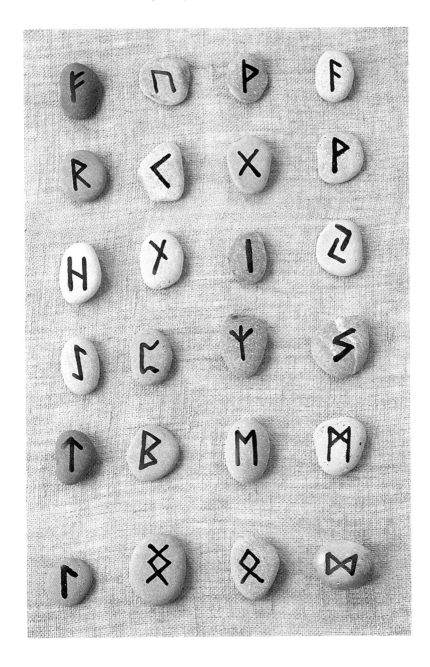

how to choose and care for runes

Many sets of runes are available, some with an accompanying book. As with any other divination technique, you need a set of runes that you will enjoy using, and whose appearance and feel you like. If you do not care for them, you will not use them. You will find a wide selection of runes for sale on the Internet, including sets made from polished crystals and pieces of metal. Some sets may have slightly different names for individual runes, depending on whether they use the Germanic or Viking names. Some of the symbols also differ according to the set you buy, which is confusing when you're still trying to remember what they all represent, but they have the same meanings. This chapter uses the Germanic names and symbols.

Traditionally, runes were made from wood, and the pictographs (symbols) were carved on them. They could also be made from stones or leather, with the glyphs painted on in blood. This added to their sacred and mysterious quality, and made them more potent for the magic in which they were often involved.

If you wish to make your own set of runes, you may draw the line at painting the glyphs in blood – a hard-wearing paint is a suitable alternative. If you enjoy carving, you could make your own runes from a hardwood. If you live near the sea, you could paint the rune symbols on small pebbles of roughly the same size. You could even make your runes from clay if you have access to a kiln. Another option is to draw the symbols on cards, to make rune cards. These are a contemporary equivalent of ancient leather runes.

Keep your runes in a bag, pouch or box. This is partly for the sake of tidiness and to keep them clean, partly because it helps to invest them with special importance. You may also like the idea of making a casting cloth for them, so that they are protected from damage when in use. The colour of the cloth should contrast with the runes so that they show up against it.

If you believe that energy can be transferred from one person to another through objects, you may like to cleanse your runes before using them for the first time. This will remove any energetic traces that have been left by other people or the manufacturing process, and is an enjoyable way to make contact with your runes. You can either wash them gently in water and pat them dry, or you can mentally cleanse them by imagining a shaft of white light passing through them. Later, when casting the runes for other people, you may wish to cleanse them after a particularly difficult reading to remove any disruptive energies. Your intuition will tell you when this is necessary.

casting the runes

The manner in which you cast the runes is entirely up to you. You can turn it into a ceremony during which you play suitable music and light candles, noting your question and the runes' answer in a book which you can refer to later. Or you may prefer to consult the runes without using any special ritual at all, simply delving into the pouch or box and taking out a rune when you need an instant answer to a question. What is important, however, is that you take the runes seriously. They will not respond in the way you wish if you treat them as a light-hearted parlour game.

The two main methods of casting runes are to place them all face down on a flat surface and select them individually, or to take one or more runes out of their container. If you choose the latter method you will soon notice how you are apparently drawn to the rune that best answers your question or reveals your state of mind.

invertible and non-invertible runes

Nine of the twenty-four runes look identical when read in their upright position or upside down. These are known as non-invertible runes. They are considered to have special power because their appearance never changes. The invertible runes have two meanings, according to whether they are upright or upside down. When they appear upside down, they have the opposite meaning to when they are the right way up. It does not automatically follow that the upright position is positive and the inverted position is negative, because some runes have very difficult upright meanings which are ameliorated when they are inverted.

Uruz normally refers to strength; when inverted it can refer to lack of energy, or to uncontrolled power.

interpreting the runes

Here are the interpretations of the individual runes, divided into the three aetts. They differ in style and tone from some of the interpretations in other chapters of this book because they approach life from a different angle. Although they can describe specific areas of life they also have a more broadly psychological slant. If you are unused to this, you may find it difficult to work with them at first but you will soon get a feel for the runes and for the deep level on which they operate. As with every other technique in this book, you need to allow your intuition to guide you and listen to your imagination if you are to get the best out of this predictive technique.

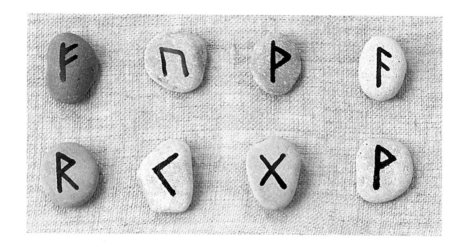

Freyja's aett

This first aett is ruled by Freyja, the Norse god of fertility. The eight runes in this aett describe creation and the basic facets of life.

Fehu

Because this rune is traditionally linked with cattle, the contemporary interpretation refers to money and possessions – cattle were once considered to be prized possessions, embodying one's wealth and ability to care for oneself and one's family. Fehu therefore not only describes money and material possessions, but also represents whatever you value in life. It sometimes asks you whether you are devoting enough time to the things and people you value most, or whether you are amassing property and money purely for the sake of it. It speaks of the need to look after and protect whatever you value, and to appreciate it fully. Fehu also has associations with food and love, because these are things that we all appreciate. When it is inverted, Fehu warns of the imminent loss of something that is valued. This might be money, possessions, health or a relationship.

Uruz

This rune is traditionally linked with aurochs, which were wild oxen. They were ferocious, horned creatures and it was considered a test of strength for young men to kill them. Therefore, this rune is connected with strength, courage and the ability to harness one's powers when confronting obstacles. It describes mental and physical stamina, and powers of endurance, all of which would have been needed when outwitting the aurochs. Uruz also represents the ability to take responsibility for your actions and to control your aggression, especially when it threatens to get out of hand. This rune may therefore describe a situation in which you need to act carefully, knowing when to retreat and when to go on the attack. When it is inverted, Uruz warns of behaving like a bull in a china shop. It can also describe a lack of energy or strength.

Thurisaz

This is a difficult rune. It is connected with Thor, the god of thunder, who was not someone you wanted to annoy. Thurisaz rules natural disasters such as earthquakes and volcanoes. Equally, this rune rules aggression, chaos, conflicts and upheavals. When this rune appears it can suggest that you will experience a situation that is the emotional or psychological equivalent of an earthquake. Although this may throw you off-balance or bring problems, it will help if you can view the situation as a catalyst that brings constructive change if handled in a positive manner. Thurisaz can also describe problems that apparently erupt without warning, such as someone deceiving you, so it counsels the need to be on your guard. When it is inverted, the negative powers of Thurisaz are greatly reduced.

Ansuz

This rune has strong links with Odin and describes the protective quality of the gods. It also describes communication in all its forms, from quick chats on the telephone to the ability to amass knowledge. It is the rune of learning, intellectual abilities and abstract ideas. Ansuz is believed to relate to gods and ancestors, and in a modern context describes people we respect and admire. It may describe a forebear, such as a grandparent, or anyone else who will pass on their wisdom or knowledge. This might be a teacher or religious leader, a mentor or father figure. In questions relating to your career, Ansuz may indicate that you will soon be given a position of authority or responsibility. Ansuz also represents the need to understand yourself and be aware of your character in all its light and shade. When this rune is inverted, it describes communication difficulties and potential problems through a generation gap.

Raido

Raido is connected with journeys of all forms, both physical and mental. It can also describe a mode of transport, such as a car or aeroplane. When interpreting this rune it is important to remember that journeys take many guises, from the literal travelling that is involved in going on holiday to the symbolic sense that life itself is a journey taking us towards an unknown destination. To develop this further, Raido can describe riding out a difficult situation in which you are able to control yourself even in adversity. It can therefore be linked with ethical behaviour and the ability to rise above problems. This carries echoes of Jung's dictum that we should control situations rather than allowing them to control us. Raido also describes taking the reins of a new project and instigating the decisions you have made. When it is inverted, Raido describes a sense of being out of control. It can also suggest that someone else is calling the shots.

Kaunaz

Traditionally, this rune is connected with pine trees, from which the Vikings cut branches to use as torches. Kaunaz therefore describes the fire of inspiration, the light of knowledge and the flames of

154

passion. When we become enthusiastic about something, we burn with ideas and energy, and this rune describes this process. However, it warns of the need to contain this energy, to channel it in productive directions and not let it burn itself out or rage out of control. Kaunaz represents knowledge, information and education, and the image of the burning torch is a reminder of the biblical entreaty to 'lighten our darkness'. It suggests shedding light on areas that have previously been dark, such as examining the hidden aspects or shadows of ourselves or others. When it is inverted, Kaunaz describes ignorance and hubris. It can also indicate a relationship that is too hot not to cool down.

Gebo

Even if you struggle to remember the names and meanings of the other runes, this one is easy. Gebo means gifts, agreements and love, and its shape suggests a kiss. It can therefore represent the gift of love, whether you are giving or receiving it. This can be a tremendous pleasure for both parties when the affections are shared, but of course there are times when love is not reciprocated and it becomes painful or frustrating. Love must also be willingly given, otherwise it has an air of coercion about it. This has echoes of the Buddhist precept that warns against taking what is not willingly offered. So sometimes this rune may refer to making emotional demands on another person, taking up too much of their time, or overwhelming them with your love. Gebo can refer to working for a higher purpose, often involving some sort of sacrifice, such as dedicating one's life to a vocation or spending a lot of time on charity work. It can represent a talent, which is another form of gift. It also describes exchanges of energy and contracts. Gebo is a non-invertible rune.

Wunjo

This is a very favourable rune because it means happiness, love, kinship and the ability to be content with your lot. It represents the sense of companionship that you experience with people who feel like kindred spirits. These may be blood relatives but may just as easily be cherished friends who feel like family. Wunjo can therefore describe the bonding that takes place when you meet people on the same wavelength as you, or who share your ideals. This rune also has links with wishes, but it reminds you that you should be careful about what you wish for because it might come true. You should make your wishes and future plans with care, and not fall into the trap of wishing for too much. If you set your sights too high you can never attain them. Wunjo is a reminder that happiness comes from accepting your current situation rather than yearning for things that may never happen. When it is inverted, Wunjo means feeling lonely and cut off from others. A wish may come to nothing.

Haegl's aett

This second aett is named after Hagalaz, the ninth rune, which describes hail and destructive winter weather. The eight runes in this aett describe forces that are beyond the control of humans. Six of them are non-invertible, suggesting the sheer power contained in this aett.

Hagalaz

Often linked to hail, Hagalaz refers to destructive forces that are beyond your control. When caught in a hailstorm, all you can do is take shelter and wait for it to pass, or grit your teeth and keep going. Therefore, Hagalaz describes difficult and unpleasant situations in which matters are taken out of your hands and you feel at the mercy of something greater than yourself. Nevertheless, good can come out of bad, so you must trust that the situation will eventually resolve itself. This rune is related to winter weather, so when caught in the grip of the disruption symbolized by this rune it is important to remember that spring always follows the ravages of winter. This is an opportunity to learn from experience and be strong in the face of adversity, rather than seeing yourself as a victim; this rune describes a test of your moral strength and courage. It may help to remember the phrase 'This too will pass.' Hagalaz is a non-invertible rune.

Nauthiz

This is a difficult rune because it means 'need'. This can be the need that we experience through lack of money or resources, or emotional needs. Need imposes limitations on us, and when we are needy we feel hemmed in and our options appear to be restricted. When we need something we have to take action, and Nauthiz encourages the sorting out of priorities and deciding how you can improve the situation in which you find yourself. This clarifies your thought processes and may even push you in a new direction. After all, necessity is the mother of invention. This rune can therefore indicate that changes are on the way, and that you will have to implement them in order to emerge from difficulties. When you find yourself in a difficult situation, try to deal with the facts and concentrate on how to solve the problem rather than wasting your energy on feeling anxious or mentally going round in circles. Nauthiz in a non-invertible rune.

Isa

The meaning of this rune can seem harsh. It represents ice, and therefore describes all the situations that occur through being in a frozen state. Just as when something frozen is in suspended animation, so Isa refers to a sense of being in limbo. Food is preserved in ice to slow down its decay, so Isa can symbolize a resistance to change and a reluctance to let life take its natural course. This may result in a need to maintain the status quo or to resist change yet be unable to move forward without it.

Alternatively, it may refer to the need for rest and recuperation after a period of hard work. Isa can represent delay, so when this rune appears your plans may be put on hold for the time being. You will have to be patient until the delay is over. Isa also describes frozen emotions, such as a sense of numbness, and frozen assets, such as problems with your cash flow. Isa is a non-invertible rune.

Jera

Jera represents the end of one cycle and the start of another. It also represents time itself, so it describes the cycle of the year in which the end leads on to a new beginning. It rules gentle changes that seem imperceptible at the time but later reveal themselves to be turning points. It is believed to have links with the Winter Solstice, after which the days gradually become longer. It can also represent karma, in which past actions influence future events, so it may warn against behaving in ways that will rebound on you later. Jera might therefore indicate the need to apologize to someone or to atone for wrong-doings or mistakes. It can also suggest a tendency to live in the past, to rehash old problems or to repeat negative patterns of behaviour. Jera also counsels patience in the knowledge that everything will eventually work out for the best. Jera is a non-invertible rune.

Eihwaz

This rune is believed to have links with yew trees and also with Yggdrasil, the tree on which Odin suspended himself for nine days and nights while waiting for enlightenment. Yew trees are traditionally planted in churchyards, so they have strong links with death. They also live for a very long time. Eihwaz's connections with yew trees and Yggdrasil therefore link it with the many mysteries associated with life and death. It also represents traits and inheritances that are passed down from one generation to the next. Because Odin's feat showed incredible stamina, Eihwaz encourages you to have endurance and willpower in the face of difficulties. Such problems may give you greater knowledge of yourself and a sense of inner stability even when times are hard. Eihwaz therefore describes tests and challenges, the ability to keep going through adversity, and great powers of endurance. Eihwaz is a non-invertible rune.

Perth

Considered one of the most mysterious runes, Perth rules the unfathomable workings of wyrd, or fate. Tradition says that a reading should be postponed if this is the first rune to be drawn, because nothing is quite what it seems. Perth encourages you to delve below the surface of things, to ignore the superficial and obvious, and to look deeply into yourself. It describes the importance of objective self-knowledge while remaining open to mysteries and inexplicable insights. It is a very creative rune and rules birth in all its forms, from a physical birth to the start of a creative project or the dawning of a talent that has remained unknown until now. This mysterious rune also has strong links with the occult, and may indicate psychic abilities. It is worth paying more attention to your dreams when Perth appears because they may help you to connect with the collective unconscious. When it is reversed, Perth describes fears which may be unfounded, and an exaggerated sensitivity to others.

Algiz

Algiz means 'protection', and it is often used for this purpose in meditation and healing. When reversed and surrounded by a circle, it is the logo for the Campaign for Nuclear Disarmament. Since the idea of protecting yourself naturally leads on to taking a defensive position, Algiz may be telling you to take better care of your health or to be more careful in any other area of your life that is under strain. It describes spiritual awareness and practice, and also refers to the relationship at the highest level between a student and teacher. Algiz may therefore mean someone who is a father figure or mentor, or who will have an important educational effect on you. It can also concern spiritual and religious aspirations, so can indicate a vocation or taking a path that will involve self-sacrifice for the greater good. When Algiz is reversed, it describes being too defensive. It can also indicate a tendency to be used by others.

Sowela

This rune is linked with the Sun. We tend to think of the Sun as a planet, but it is really a star and the centre of our solar system. Without its light and heat we would perish. Sowela therefore represents energy and power. We need these to make things happen, and Sowela is encouraging you to be enthusiastic and to have faith in yourself. This rune offers protection and encouragement when times are difficult, and urges you to keep going when you feel like giving up. It promises eventual success and justified pride in your achievements. Because Sowela is full of warmth and optimism, it brightens up any reading and provides a welcome balance if any of the challenging runes appear alongside it. It also refers to good health, so it offers reassurance and the prospect of healing if you are ill or convalescing. Sowela is a non-invertible rune.

Tyr's aett

The third aett is named after Tyr, who is believed to have been a god of justice or war. He has links with Teiwaz, the seventeenth rune. The eight runes in this aett describe transformation and the human condition.

Teiwaz

Tyr, after whom this rune was named, was a warrior god. He lost his right hand in punishment for swearing a false oath, and there is an element of justice bordering on retribution with this rune. Viking warriors used to carve this rune on their bracelets before going into battle. Teiwaz can therefore confer victory, courage and strength of purpose, offering encouragement when you are about to face a difficult or highly challenging situation. Warriors need leadership in battle, and Teiwaz describes the ability to harness your resources and take command. It also denotes bravery, honour and the ability to stand up for yourself. Very often, Teiwaz rules battles that are fought for the good of everyone, such as an environmental campaign or a human rights issue. There is an element of competitiveness here, so this rune describes all forms of competition, especially those concerning sport and business. When it is inverted, Teiwaz indicates a defeat of some kind.

Berkana

Strong links with fertility connect this rune with pregnancy. It can describe the birth of a child but also relates to birth on a wider scale, such as the birth of an idea, a project or a new chapter in your life. It is an especially favourable rune for creative projects. Anything that is just beginning needs careful nurturing if it is going to survive, so nurturing is another meaning of Berkana. It can describe looking after people, especially children. If you are unwell, Berkana indicates the need for healing and recuperation. In its guise as the fertility rune, Berkana rules trees and plants, and may therefore suggest the need to become more involved with nature or cultivate a garden as a means of rejuvenation and enjoyment. When things are gestating they are hidden from the world, and Berkana can describe secrets that have yet to see the light of day. When it is inverted, Berkana means an inability to grow, whether symbolically or literally. It can also describe a difficult transition from one stage in life to the next.

Ehwaz

Be careful not to confuse this rune with Eihwaz, which belongs in the second aett. Ehwaz is said to have strong links with horses. In Viking times horses were used for travelling, so travel can be indicated when this rune appears. This travel may be a holiday, a house move or even emigration. But its equine meaning goes further than simple travel because any journey would be a misery, and possibly even dangerous, without a rapport between horse and rider. Ehwaz therefore describes the importance of establishing a partnership with someone or something, in which both parties have much to contribute. It can also describe friendship, and especially a relationship in which one person has the upper hand, such as the link between boss and employee. Co-operation, flexibility and understanding are all needed when this rune appears. When it is inverted, Ehwaz means a betrayal of trust and an inability to co-operate.

Mannaz

This rune is linked to humans, particularly our ability to think and reason. It describes correct human behaviour, so it relates to decency, politeness, co-operation and consideration for others. Mannaz also describes how others see us and their attitude towards us. Such people can be friends or enemies. If you are experiencing relationship problems and this rune appears in a reading, it may be a gentle reminder of the part your own motives and behaviour have played in the situation and that you should not simply point the finger of blame at the other person. Mannaz also suggests that you should review past relationships to see if you are repeating a pattern. It therefore describes the ability to keep an open mind and approach situations with intelligence and objectivity. It is a very positive rune if you are embarking on a spiritual or educational path. It can also offer encouragement if you are involved in a legal matter. When it is inverted, Mannaz describes bigotry and a closed mind. This is someone who thinks they have all the answers and refuses to acknowledge anyone else's point of view.

Laguz

Psychotherapy draws links between water and the unconscious, and as Laguz relates to water it describes the ability to tune into your unconscious and intuition. This makes it an excellent rune to draw when embarking upon some form of psychic development, but it also suggests using your intuition in less structured ways such as simply trusting your gut instincts. It will be helpful to pay extra attention to your dreams as they may send you vivid messages or illustrations of the current state of your mind and emotions. Laguz has powerful occult links and can hint that certain things are hidden at the moment. Laguz also describes the power of imagination, making it good for creative projects. We use water for cleaning and to flush things through, so this is a suitable rune for some form of spiritual or physical cleansing. On a more mundane level, Laguz can describe a steady stream of something, such as money, friends or emotions. When it is inverted, Laguz describes emotional blackmail and allowing yourself to be overwhelmed by fear.

Inguz

This rune has strong connections with fertility and is therefore linked with Freyja, the fertility god. It describes the seed stage, when projects and relationships are starting to germinate. It therefore has links with agriculture, horticulture and nature in general. It can describe the ability to live in harmony with nature and with the rhythm of the seasons. Inguz also describes human fertility and gestation, and may therefore foretell the birth of a child. Inguz refers to fruitfulness in more general terms, too, such as spawning a new creative project, beginning a venture that will be prosperous or embarking on a successful relationship. It also encourages you to be more appreciative of the richness of life during those times when you feel downhearted or depressed, and life does not seem to have much to offer. Inguz is a non-invertible rune.

Othila

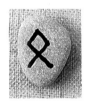

Links with all forms of inheritance, whether financial, genetic, cultural or historical, mean that Othila may describe property, possessions or money that has been passed down to us. It can also refer to the codes of behaviour and values that families try to instil in their offspring. Sometimes, Othila can describe a strong emotional link between a child and a parent or grandparent. It may also refer to inherited health problems, or to gifts and talents that we inherit from our forebears. To take this meaning further, Othila describes a sense of connection with our ancestors and the place where they lived – it is evoked when people speak longingly of 'the old country'. When Othila is inverted, it can indicate a rigid clinging to a past way of life or a refusal to accept progress and change. It may also refer to unfulfilled expectations of an inheritance.

Dagaz

This rune means 'day'. When the Sun rises it is the start of another day and the chance for something new to happen. Dagaz therefore refers to beginnings and a fresh chapter in your life. It is the companion rune to Jera because it describes the Summer Solstice, when we have the maximum amount of daylight. It therefore represents all forms of enlightenment. This may be the mental enlightenment that comes when you see things in a new light, or spiritual enlightenment when you gain insights into the nature of life. Dagaz also signifies the light at the end of the tunnel when you are emerging from a period of depression or illness and hope is dawning once more. The Summer Solstice marks a turning point in the Sun's path, and Dagaz can therefore represent fundamental changes and transformations from one stage to another. In times of trouble, this rune offers reassurance that things will get better. Dagaz is a non-invertible rune.

the blank rune

Opinion is divided about whether the blank rune or wyrd belongs in a set of runes. Many traditional runecasters believe it is a heresy and should be completely ignored. However, the decision is yours. Of course, it will depend initially on whether your set of runes contains a blank rune. If it does, you might like to work with it at first to see whether it has any significance for you. You may find it adds nothing to your readings, in which case you may choose to abandon it.

Devotees of the blank rune say it is connected with karma and complete change. It has a similar meaning to the Death card in the tarot, indicating that some form of psychological death will take place. This may be a transformation from one stage of life to the next, or it might indicate that a radical decision is needed.

When the blank rune is drawn in a Single Rune Reading, it is telling you that this is not a good time to ask your question. This could be for one of many reasons. For instance, the situation may be about to change or the question may now be redundant although you do not yet know it. Ask your question a few days later, if it is still relevant.

single rune reading

When you first begin working with runes you may feel unsure of your ability to interpret them properly. It will therefore help to begin practising with elementary readings. For a Single Rune Reading you simply place all the runes in a pouch and then draw out a single one. Think of a particular question or ask for general guidance while you do this. If the rune is invertible, it will be inverted if it is upside down when you look at it as soon as you have taken it out of the pouch. If you are looking at the blank back of the rune, turn it over without turning it upside down.

Sally wanted a very simple reading when she was considering moving house. She was unsure whether she was doing the right thing and whether she would be as happy in her prospective new home as she was in her current one. The rune she selected was Gebo. This means a gift or an exchange of some kind, so clearly described an exchange of contracts on the property, and the happiness that would follow in Sally's new location.

past, present and future spread

This is a classic runic spread. Indeed, you will find similar spreads in other divination techniques, such as the tarot and cartomancy. Its beauty lies in its simplicity. You can always draw further runes to expand the meaning of each category if you wish for more enlightenment.

To select the three runes, you can either take them out of the pouch and place them in the correct order in front of you, or you can place all the runes face down in front of you, swirl them around and pick the three that most attract you.

This particular reading was given to Beth, who wanted to gain some insight into the general pattern of her life. She had recently become self-employed because her previous job had been too demanding. She felt that she was not yet fulfilling her potential and hoped that the runes would give her some guidance about how to remedy this. The three runes that Beth drew are linked by the themes of fertility and creativity, thus echoing the nature of her question.

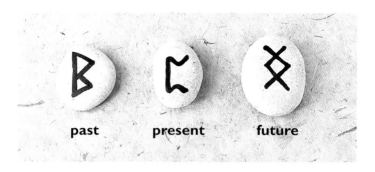

past Berkana This very positive rune shows that Beth began a new chapter in her life when she became self-employed. It also shows that she needed to recuperate after a very busy phase. It hints at abilities within Beth that have yet to be expressed.

present Perth Perhaps Beth should rely on her intuition to steer her in the right direction? She had been toying with the idea of training to be a psychotherapist, and Perth has strong links with such disciplines. It seems she is thinking along the right lines.

future Inguz Whatever path Beth decides to follow, this rune reassures her that things will go well and she will gain the creative satisfaction she craves.

options spread

This is an excellent spread when you have to make a difficult choice and want to examine your options. Before you start, think clearly about the situation and the choices you have to make, then write them down so that you know which option represents which choice. In theory, you can have up to twelve choices, although in practice this may become unwieldy and you may find it easier to examine only two or three choices at a time.

For instance, if you have been offered two jobs and are unsure about which one to take, you can lay out two runes for the first job and two for the second. You then interpret the message given by each set of runes. Using two runes for each option expands the interpretation and describes the situation in more detail. Once you become used to runes you will find it easy to combine the meanings of two runes.

Choose the runes in either of the ways described above – either by taking them out of a bag or by choosing runes that have been placed face down on a flat surface.

This reading was for Sarah, who was strongly attracted to two men, Jeff and Dave, but did not know which one was right for her. Jeff is charismatic and self-assured, with a slight aura of danger, and Dave is intense and somewhat withdrawn. Jeff was represented by the first option and Dave by the second.

first option Raido and Kaunaz This option represents Jeff. Raido is connected with journeys, whether on a spiritual, mental, physical or emotional level. Kaunaz is linked with inspiration and passion. Together, they are a very exciting combination and show that a relationship with Jeff would be an unforgettable experience in which Sarah could learn a great deal. The most striking aspect of this combination is that both runes describe the need for control over oneself and over situations. Sarah admitted that she felt a relationship with Jeff might easily become too much for her to cope with, and the prospect unnerved her.

second option Gebo and Wunjo This option represents Dave. Gebo describes gifts, love and agreements. Wunjo is connected with happiness and wishes. The combination is a delightful one, suggesting joy, contentment and a deep emotional link. It indicates that a relationship with Dave would bring great happiness. Sarah smiled wryly when she was told that Wunjo warns against wishing for the unattainable; she admitted that she would like Dave to have some of Jeff's exciting qualities. She realized, however, that she was trying to turn Dave into something he was not and

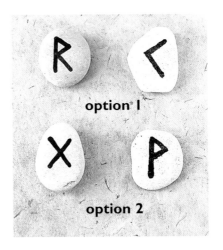

option 1

option 2

that she should appreciate him for what he was. Sarah decided to pursue her relationship with him.

dominoes

The art of using dominoes to tell your fortune comes under the category of cleromancy, which means using small objects for divination purposes. It is amusing to think that the box of dominoes so often dragged out to keep children quiet at Christmas can be used to discover your fortune.

The origin of dominoes is uncertain, but they are believed to have been invented in China as far back as the twelfth century AD. It is thought that they were developed from dice, which had been introduced from India a long time before. They represented the twenty-one different results of throwing two dice, with one half of the tile showing the spots on one dice and the other half showing the spots on the other. Chinese dominoes gradually spawned mah-jongh, a game that uses similar tiles. Dominoes appeared in the West around the early eighteenth century, when they became popular in Italy. From here they spread to France and Britain.

By this time European dominoes differed from their original Chinese form. They no longer simply represented the different results of throwing two dice. They now had seven extra dominoes, six of them the result of throwing one dice accompanied by a blank. The seventh domino was a double blank. This is known as the double-six set. Today, domino sets have evolved still further and you can buy double-twelve sets of ninety-one dominoes. Luckily for us, these are not used for predictive work!

Although dominoes are known primarily as a game, they have a long tradition of being used to tell fortunes, especially in Korea and India. Some domino games in India and China even combine gambling and divination.

Dominoes have a very direct quality. Unlike the tarot, there are no pictures to stimulate your intuition and no deep symbolism to trace back to other esoteric techniques. You simply work with a collection of tiles studded with a variety of spots. If you wish, you can use the nearest domino set to hand, or buy a special one that you use exclusively for fortune telling.

fortune telling with dominoes

Traditional sources say that you should not read dominoes too
often because they can give conflicting messages. You may also
find it best to read them only once at each
session. If you decide to give yourself two
readings, take note of the dominoes that appear
the first time round. If a domino appears in the
second reading, too, its meaning is accentuated.

If you want to reserve a set of dominoes
specifically for divination, keep them in a special
bag or box, rather than the box they came in.
You may also enjoy placing them on a special
cloth when giving a reading, to accentuate their
importance. All this will become part of the
ritual that will help you to focus on the
divination about to take place.

giving a reading

There are two traditional ways of reading dominoes. You can either
draw a single domino to answer a question, or you can choose
three dominoes to represent different facets of your life. For
instance, if you want to know whether a love affair will work out
well, you might prefer to draw one domino. However, if you want
an insight into several areas of your life, such as your past, present
and future, you can draw three dominoes and assign one to each
category. Reading any more than three dominoes at one time can
become confusing, but this is entirely a matter of choice. You may
feel quite confident about using ten dominoes for a complex
reading simply because you have a strong affinity with them.

Some authorities recommend removing all seven dominoes
that feature blanks before giving a reading, but this is up to you.
Place all the dominoes face down on the table or on your special
piece of cloth. Spend a few moments consciously relaxing, so you
are prepared for the reading. Think of the question you want to ask
the dominoes and keep it in your mind. If you are giving someone
else a reading, ask them to think of their question. Swirl the
dominoes around slowly with the palms of your hands to mix them

up thoroughly, while thinking of your question. Stop moving the dominoes around when your intuition tells you they are in position. Choose one or more dominoes, turn them over and interpret them in the light of the question that has been asked.

These dominoes indicate a very busy time ahead.

the interpretations

Here are the traditional interpretations of the twenty-eight dominoes of the standard double-six set.

Six-six

This is the luckiest domino in the set. It indicates that happiness and success are on the way. Very often it also refers to financial or material prosperity. This is the emotional equivalent of throwing a double-six with dice – there is something to celebrate.

Six-five

This tile is connected with close friends. They may be very supportive or repay you for a previous act of kindness. There can also be a change of status, such as someone marrying or becoming a parent.

Six-four

There may be a disagreement or quarrel but it is unlikely to have dire consequences. When it takes place between close friends it can lead them to a better understanding of one another. Occasionally, however, this tile can indicate an unsuccessful lawsuit. It is certainly a time to be aware of your actions.

Six-three

Travel is indicated, whether for business or pleasure. The journey will have a powerful impact on you, perhaps because it introduces you to important new contacts or because you visit a country that will have great significance. If this tile refers to a long-awaited holiday, it will fulfil all your expectations.

Six-two

Provided you act in good faith and do nothing for which you should reproach yourself, you will receive some tremendous opportunities. You may even receive a windfall or gift. However, past misdeeds will come back to haunt you if you have not been honest with someone.

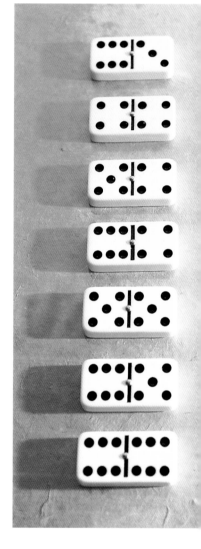

Six-one

Traditionally, this tile denotes a wedding. It can also represent making some other vow or form of emotional commitment, such as an engagement or spiritual vow. If you have been facing problems recently they may now come to a conclusion, especially with the help of a good friend.

Six-blank

This tile warns against gossip, especially from so-called friends. They may give you false information or be talking about you behind your back. Equally, you should be wary of saying things that are better left unsaid, so try to keep your thoughts to yourself for the time being. Otherwise, something you say might be used against you.

Five-five

Change is on the way, and it is important to be receptive to it when it arrives. If you are resistant and wish to cling to the status quo, you will encounter many difficulties. You may already know that things are changing, so take comfort from the knowledge that the end results will be beneficial.

Five-four

Money is on the way and is most likely to arrive in the form of a windfall from an official source, such as a tax rebate or dividend from an investment. Although money may be coming in, this is not a good time for lavish spending or reckless gambles. Be prudent and avoid taking financial risks.

Five-three

Everything is going well! This tile indicates a period of calm and contentment in all areas of your life, plus possible financial prosperity. Friends and colleagues are keen to help you when necessary. You may also benefit from someone's advice and a visitor may bring news.

Five-two

The traditional meaning of this tile is birth. This may refer to someone else's child or your own. It also refers to a deep friendship, especially if this friend gives you good advice or administers a gentle warning. It can therefore indicate a highly enjoyable social phase. Sometimes, it may also counsel the virtues of patience and tolerance.

Five-one

This will be a hectic time socially, with plenty of invitations and outings. There is also the possibility of a new love affair that starts in a rush of excitement and pleasure but which can end in less positive ways. When entering a love affair now, it is advisable to take things slowly.

Five-blank

Be careful! This tile warns of the need for caution, particularly in financial matters, if you want to avoid making mistakes. A friend may need your help in solving a problem and will value your compassionate input. Nevertheless, you may have to choose your words carefully and exercise considerable tact.

Four-four

This very positive domino indicates a period of fun, happiness, sociability and general wellbeing. It is telling you to put work commitments to one side whenever possible, and to concentrate on the lighter side of life. Go with the flow, rather than trying to control what happens.

Four-three

If life has been bleak recently or you are fearful of something, this tile offers hope in the face of considerable odds. Things will not be nearly as dire as you suspect, and life may even start to improve in unexpected ways. It will help to adopt a positive attitude while still recognizing potential trouble-spots.

Four-two

Changes are on the way that will usually bring improvements in your life. There may be an element of surprise, though, with the changes coming from unexpected directions. Take care when handling your finances and be extremely wary of anyone who is untrustworthy or even dishonest.

Four-one

Take considerable care over your finances. Money may soon be rather thin on the ground, or you may be saddled with many outgoings. Tradition says it is important to settle your debts while you can afford it, in order to avoid problems later on. Debts aside, you should be saving money right now, not spending it.

Four-blank

This domino indicates difficulties and disruptions, especially in your relationships. There may be a quarrel, particularly over secrets that have been betrayed or divulged. Therefore, it might be wise to think twice before confiding in someone. There can also be delays in getting plans off the ground.

Three-three

Your financial situation will soon improve dramatically, with large amounts of money on the way. These may arrive from several sources. The situation is not so fortunate in emotional matters, perhaps because someone is jealous of your affluent status. This is a time when love and money definitely do not mix.

Three-two

This tile warns against taking chances in love, money and health. However, if you heed this advice you can look forward to an enjoyable time. It is especially favourable for making careful investments. Travel plans will be successful and close relationships will go through a very satisfying phase.

Three-one

Be very wary about too much involvement with others. For example, they may interfere with your plans in some way, give you imprudent advice or cause problems through gossip. Traditionally, if you have asked the dominoes a question, three-one gives a negative answer.

Three-blank

This is a difficult tile because it warns of arguments and disputes that seem to come out of the blue. In fact, they have probably been building up for some time but you have been unaware of them. There may also be problems with a partner who behaves foolishly or irresponsibly.

Two-two

This is one of the most favourable tiles to draw because it indicates professional success and personal happiness. You will be most productive in your career and business concerns if you take things at a slow and steady pace. The only snag is possible jealousy from people who want what you have.

Two-one

Financial arrangements could be put in jeopardy, perhaps because of your association with certain people. On a positive note, this tile indicates very happy friendships and may even refer to a relationship that will bring material benefits. Sometimes there may be a reunion with an old friend.

Two-blank

Travel looks excellent and may even introduce you to someone who will be important in your life. If you are currently plagued by worries and anxieties, this tile is telling you to analyse them with as much objectivity as possible. A change of scene may help to put things in perspective.

One-one

This tile indicates harmony and happiness in every area of your life. Problems will be alleviated and may even be solved without any effort on your part. Do not delay in making an important decision – this is no time for procrastination. Trust that you will choose the best option.

One-blank

Do not be too trusting of people, especially if you barely know them. It is important to remember this if a stranger or acquaintance brings you financial news that appears to work in your favour. If something sounds too good to be true, that is probably exactly what it is! Be wary.

Blank-blank

This is the least favourable domino because it describes difficult outcomes and severe disappointments. You may feel as though you have hit rock bottom. Try to be aware of your behaviour because you will reap what you sow. You may even feel that any difficulties you encounter are the results of previous actions.

domino readings

Sarah asked whether to buy an expensive new car. As this question required a simple answer, she drew a single domino from the bag in which they were kept. The tile she chose was Five-blank, which warned her to be careful when spending money. She took this as an unequivocal 'no' to her question.

Dave was interested to know what was happening in his life. He was considering changing his job because he was having so many personality clashes with his boss. However, he was not sure whether the problems lay with his difficult boss or were caused by his own behaviour. He laid out the dominoes, face down, in front of him and chose three to represent his past, present and future. For the past, he chose Three-blank. This tile describes arguments and disputes, and he admitted that he used to be a difficult person to get along with because he often provoked disagreements. For the present, he chose Two-one which describes problems in relationships based on financial arrangements. He took this to mean the difficulties with his boss. However, he was pleased by the description of happy friendships, which implied that even if he had been awkward in the past he had now moved beyond this. For the future, he selected Three-one. This domino advises being careful about mixing with other people, which Dave took as a warning not to spend much longer in his current job. He had been considering becoming self-employed and interpeted this reading as a favourable sign that this would suit him.

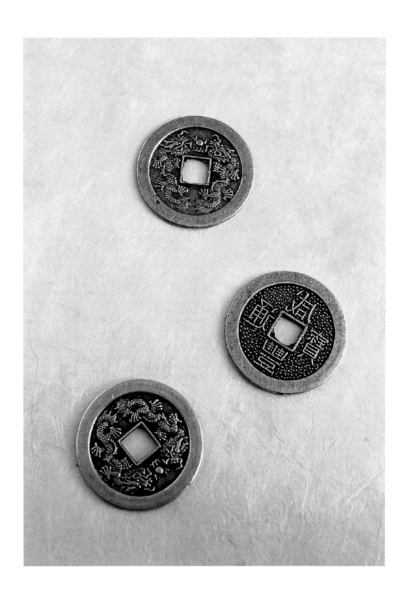

i ching

The literal translation of the I Ching is the 'Book of Changes'
because it was written to reflect the many changes that take
place in our lives and throughout the universe. The I Ching
reminds us that nothing stays static. Happiness comes and gives
way to sorrow. Sorrow comes and gives way to happiness.
Prosperity may be superseded by penury and penury by
prosperity. Everything passes in time.

The exact origins of the I Ching are buried deep in Chinese history. Nevertheless, it is believed to have developed from the ancient practice of burning animal bones and tortoise shells, and the interpretion of the cracks that appeared because of the intense heat. In time, the patterns created by the cracks were translated into the eight basic trigrams, or figures consisting of three lines, that we still use today in the I Ching.

Around 1150 BC the Shang dynasty was drawing to a close under the rulership of the Emperor, Chou Hsin. A provincial noble called Wên had the misfortune of being a great deal more popular than the Emperor, who retaliated by throwing him in prison. While he was there, Wên studied the trigrams, pairing them up in every possible permutation to create the sixty-four hexagrams that we know today. He then wrote a commentary to accompany each hexagram. In time, Wên's son, Tan, the Duke of Chou, continued his father's work on the hexagrams, interpreting each line within each hexagram. After this, Confucius and his later disciples added their own contributions. The I Ching soon became a divination classic and also a spiritual guide. It managed to escape destruction in 213 BC when many ancient books were burned under the orders of the emperor – only books on divination, farming and medicine were saved. Between 3 BC and 3 AD magicians revised the I Ching in their search for immortality. The version we are familiar with today was largely created by the scholar Wang Pi, late in 3 AD.

Although the I Ching has been published in the West since the 1880s, it really only became popular because of Carl Jung's enthusiasm for it in the early twentieth century. In the past, many people were deterred from consulting it because of the way it was written, with its references to Chinese life thousands of years ago. The images, which included emperors and animals, were often hard to relate to contemporary life and therefore offputting. Today, however, you can buy many translations of the I Ching that vary from the easily read to the dense and scholarly. There are even CD-ROMs in which all the hard work is done for you; all you need do is ask a question and read the interpretation.

consulting the I Ching

As with every other divination technique in this book, the
I Ching will respond in the same spirit with which you consult it.
If you consider it to be a game or something to help you pass
the time, it will never give you reason to change your mind.
However, if you consult it with reverence and respect you will
appreciate its many benefits and will come to rely on it when
you need impartial yet profound advice.

It is important to phrase your question in a way
that can easily be answered by the I Ching. Either/or
questions, such as 'Should I go to the party or
should I go to the cinema?' are not appropriate.
Break the question into two separate questions
('What will happen if I go to the party?', and 'What
will happen if I go to the cinema?') and throw a
hexagram for each one. You can then compare the
two answers and make your decision accordingly.

When you are confident that you have chosen a suitable
question, write it down. This fixes it in your mind and prevents
the temptation to alter it slightly once you have seen the
I Ching's answer! Keep the paper next to you because you will
draw the hexagram on it. If you enjoy working with the I Ching
you can record your sessions in a special notebook, in which case
it will be very useful to write the question next to the hexagram,
possibly adding the time and date.

You build up a hexagram, which is the key to your reading, by
throwing particular objects six times. Each time you either draw
a solid line or a broken line on a piece of paper, according to the
value of the throw. After the sixth throw, you will have
constructed a hexagram and can then read its interpretation in
the list that appears later in this chapter. You build the hexagram
from the bottom up, so the result of the first throw forms its
bottom line and the sixth throw forms its top line.

One of the traditional ways to consult the I Ching is to throw
fifty yarrow stalks and use the results to build the hexagram.
However, this is an extremely complex method, and you may be
irritated to discover that you do not have the required yarrow

stalks just when you need them. It is much easier to use three coins of the same denomination and size. This is another traditional way to consult the I Ching, although special Chinese coins with one inscribed and one blank side were originally used. If you wish to create a sense of ritual around the I Ching, you may prefer to find three foreign coins which are only used for this purpose. Alternatively, you can delve into your pocket for loose change whenever you want to consult the I Ching. It is entirely a matter of personal choice.

Decide which side of the coin is the equivalent of the inscribed side (usually the one showing the denomination). This will have a value of two. The reverse side has a value of three. Hold the coins in your hands or place them in a cup, fix the question in your mind and throw the coins on to a level surface. Note the value of each coin and count them up to give a total. Even totals (six or eight) are written as a yin line, which is a broken line. Odd totals (seven or nine) are written as a yang line, which is a solid line. Remember that you build the hexagram from the bottom up, so the first throw gives you the bottom line of the hexagram. Draw the line on the piece of paper. Now throw the coins again, count up their value and draw the appropriate line above the bottom line of the hexagram. Continue like this until you have six lines, which form your hexagram.

Inscribed side = 2
Reverse side = 3
Even number = broken yin line
Odd number = solid yang line

This chapter contains a simplified version of the I Ching because of lack of space, but you will find a more complicated procedure in any classic I Ching book. This involves the use of so-called 'moving lines' that are calculated in a slightly different way to the one described above. You read the completed hexagram, with interpretations of these individual moving lines, and then convert any moving lines to their opposite, so broken lines become solid, and vice versa. This gives you a second hexagram to read, after which you refer to the interpretations of the individual moving lines.

a sample reading

The question is 'What will happen if I try to rekindle my broken relationship with Jenny?' The first throw gives three reversed sides, which add up to nine. This provides a solid line for the bottom line of the hexagon. The second throw also gives three reversed sides, adding up to nine, so the fifth line is also solid. The third throw gives one inscribed and two reversed sides, which add up to eight. The fourth line is therefore written as a broken line. The fourth throw gives three inscribed sides, which add up to six and are drawn as a broken line. The fifth throw gives two inscribed and one reversed sides, adding up to seven. This is drawn as a solid line. The final throw gives three inscribed sides, which add up to six and are shown by a broken line.

The next step is to look up the hexagram in the following table so you can easily locate it in the interpretation list. Separate it into its two trigrams by drawing an imaginary division between the third and fourth lines. This gives you an upper trigram of one solid line enclosed between two broken lines, and a lower trigram of one broken line above two solid lines.

Turn to the trigram key overleaf and look along the horizontal row to find the upper trigram. You will see that it is called K'an. Now look down the vertical row to find the lower trigram. You will see that it is called Tui. Now look for the square where these two rows meet. It contains the number sixty, and this is the number of the hexagram that answers the question. All you need do now is turn to this hexagram in the list.

This hexagram is called Limitation. It describes the need to place sensible limitations and restrictions on oneself, suggesting

**Consulting the I Ching using foreign coins that you keep
exclusively for that purpose may add to the sense of ritual.**

that it is not a good idea to try and mend the broken
relationship. At this point you need to consider why the
relationship with Jenny ended in the first place. It was because
she was very bossy and possessive, and this is reflected in the
latter part of the interpretation that warns against allowing
others to impose restrictions on oneself. The I Ching is clearly
advising against rekindling this relationship.

trigram key

lower trigram		Ch'ien	Chên	K'an
	Ch'ien	1	34	5
	Chên	25	51	3
	K'an	6	40	29
	Kên	33	62	39
	K'un	12	16	8
	Sun	44	32	48
	Li	13	55	63
	Tui	10	54	60

t r i g r a m

Kên	**K'un**	**Sun**	**Li**	**Tui**
26	11	9	14	43
27	24	42	21	17
4	7	59	64	47
52	15	53	56	31
23	2	20	35	45
18	46	57	50	28
22	36	37	30	49
41	19	61	38	58

the sixty-four hexagrams

Here are the interpretations of the hexagrams. Their Chinese name is given in addition to their number and their English name.

1 **Ch'ien** Creativity

Everything is going well. If you continue on your current course you will be heading for success. Creative ventures will be especially successful.

2 **K'un** Devotion

Your efforts will bring you tremendous success provided that you follow the path that has been set for you, and do not stray from it. It is better to be a devoted follower at the moment.

3 **Chun** A Difficult Start

Despite a difficult start your venture will lead to success. Do not be tempted to change direction or alter your plans, but continue in your current course. Nevertheless, you may wish to ask for help.

4 **Mêng** Inexperience

Be prepared to give someone the benefit of your advice and experience, and encourage them to have faith that all will be well. Listen to the wisdom of the I Ching, but do not rely on it to answer every question you may have.

5 **Hsü** Patience

Do not rush into anything in haste. You must cultivate patience, resolution and the ability to conserve your energy. If you wait for the right time to act, major changes or big plans will be very successful. Choose your time carefully.

6 **Sung** Conflict

Be very careful when handling a quarrel or disagreement. Even though you know you are in the right, the odds are stacked against you. It is important to reach a compromise and not to pursue a policy of vengeance because that will only lead to retribution and further difficulties.

7 **Shih** The Army

You need to take command of the current situation, marshalling your defences and being thoroughly organized. If you are not in control of yourself you cannot expect to succeed. Draw on your wisdom and experience, and make sure your strategy is feasible.

8 **Pi** Working in Unison

United action is much more productive than a solitary effort now. You will be much more effective when you are part of a team, but do not delay in setting this in motion. Consult the I Ching again if necessary to see if you will take a leadership role or be part of the group.

9 **Hsiao Ch'u** Restraint

Hold back. You will have far more success if you adopt a gentle, restrained approach than if you go in with all guns blazing. The end is within sight but has not yet arrived. You must be patient and wait for ultimate success.

10 **Lü** Treading Carefully

Even when dealing with a difficult or dangerous situation, you will not come to harm if you tread carefully and warily. You may even make some very intrepid or daring moves and still escape peril, provided you take things very gently and behave with propriety.

11 **T'ai** Peace

Petty problems and other minor irritations are fading from sight, so calm will prevail. You will enjoy some peaceful progress and prosperity as your stock starts to rise and you feel more sure of yourself. This can eventually lead to great success.

12 **P'i** Stagnation

A stand-off looks likely because you are facing opposition from people who are small-minded and petty. They are not big enough to cope with the current situation. You may also find yourself being sucked into spats and squabbles that lead to a stalemate when no one is seen at their best.

13 **T'ung Jên** Comradeship

There is no room for the ego in harmonious and productive relationships. Do not imagine that you are bigger than a particular relationship, or act for selfish reasons. Success will come through being honest, straightforward and honourable.

14 **Ta Yu** Wealth

You are heading towards success and prosperity. Wealth will be available to you in many forms, not only materially but in other ways too. Although you will have good reason to feel pleased with your progress, it will not turn your head or make you become self-important.

15 **Ch'ien** Modesty

Adopt a modest and moderate approach for maximum success. It is far better to cultivate humility than to become puffed up with your own importance, which could lead to opposition or hubris. Even if you occupy a position of great authority, it will benefit you to maintain a humble and modest attitude.

16 **Yü** Enthusiasm

If you are struggling to put a plan into action or make a success of something, it may help to enlist the support and help of other people. In order to do this, your enthusiasm for the project must be so infectious that your helpers become equally enthused.

17 **Sui** Following

Follow your conscience because it will tell you how best to behave in the current circumstances. If you act in ways that you know are wrong or which prick your conscience, you will encounter opposition and trouble. It is important that you set a good example.

18 **Ku** Decay

You need to repair the problems caused by previous mistakes. However, this is not something you should rush into. Think things through for three days before repairing the damage and spend the following three days actively working to make sure it does not happen again.

19 **Lin** Approaches

Adopting the correct approach pays off now by bringing you success and happiness. However, remember that everything in life changes, and that this success will eventually give way to difficult circumstances.

20 **Kuan** Contemplation

Consider the natural order of the world – the seasons come and go in an endless cycle. Wisdom is attained by accepting that life consists of this cycle and that it cannot be changed. Do not waste time trying to change anything that is immovable or beyond your control.

21 **Shih Ho** Biting Through

You need to overcome obstacles and problems in order to achieve success. This will not be a pleasant or easy process, but it is necessary. You may be involved in some form of legal process in order to restrain someone or defend your rights.

22 **Pi** Beauty

Beauty is only skin deep. An attractive appearance may mask an unattractive nature. This is a good time to improve your image or enhance your appearance but do not become obsessed by your looks. When making plans, concentrate on their essence and do not be sidetracked by superficial details.

23 **Po** Falling Apart

Something is coming to an end, and may even collapse entirely. You must allow this process to be completed before you can start anything new. In the meantime, people may show themselves to be mean-spirited but do not let yourself be one of them.

24 **Fu** Returning

The natural order of things is changing once again, allowing a more productive time to ensue. You will no longer feel you are fighting against the odds. The situation will improve and you will revisit previous successes. You may want to give a difficult problem or relationship one last chance, and this time it will go well.

25 **Wu Wang** Honesty

It is essential that you act with honesty and integrity. If you can behave in an honourable way, even in the face of opposition, you will achieve success and power. However, if you do not behave this way you will find it very hard to extricate yourself from the ensuing difficult situation, and will make no progress in any direction.

26 **Ta Ch'u** Gaining by Restraint

You will benefit by being firm and acting properly. This is not a good time to restrict yourself to your usual circle of associates – you will fare better if you spread your net more widely and work with a greater number of people. This is an especially favourable time for overseas travel.

27 **I** Gaining Nourishment

If you are wise, you will nourish others as well as yourself. Carefully consider nourishment in all its forms, spiritual, mental and emotional as well as physical. Give other people and yourself the nourishment needed, but be moderate.

28 **Ta Kuo** Excessiveness

A situation is becoming far too stressful for you to tolerate. If you allow things to continue as they are, there will be some sort of collapse. You must act quickly to prevent this happening. It may help to confide in someone or to ask their advice.

29 **K'an** The Abyss

You are currently experiencing a perilous situation, but you will survive it if you can keep your head and do not lose sight of the facts. It will help to understand the difference between problems that are mere obstacles and those that are beyond your control. Proceed with honesty and all will be well.

30 **Li** Fire

People depend on you, just as you depend on others. Understand that your existence is dependent on many things beyond yourself, and trust that you will receive the help that you need. There is little use in fighting against the natural order of life because it is more mysterious than you can imagine.

31 **Hsien** Attraction

You are very attracted to someone, and they to you. Nevertheless, you should allow events to proceed at their own pace and for nature to take its course, rather than trying to speed things up. Consider the other person's feelings before your own.

32 **Hêng** Duration

You will be successful if you stand firm and behave well. Continue with the present situation because that is the best route to success and prosperity. Proceed with your plans because they will go well.

33 **Tun** Retreat

This is a good moment to retreat, not through weakness but because it will be the most successful tactic in the long run. It is important to retreat at the right time though. After you have retreated, concentrate on the details of your plans and do not try to force the issue.

34 **Ta Chuang** Strength

Do not confuse might with right. You have tremendous strength of purpose, but this will be worth nothing if you use it to succeed in activities that harm others or bring trouble. The means do not justify the ends. Combine your current strength with honourable behaviour, and you will gain insight into the nature of life.

35 **Chin** Progress

This hexagram describes the story of a successful prince who is presented with many horses and has three audiences with the king in a single day. If you act for other people's welfare as well as your own, you will be successful and will receive unexpected gifts and worldly attention.

36 **Ming I** Quenching of the Light

You have reached a point where it is politic to be modest about your achievements, and to put your ambitions to one side for the sake of prudence. Provided you remain aware of your abilities you will not be diminished by your current subservient or modest position.

37 **Chia Jên** The Family

Fulfil your proper role within your family or group. Do not try to be something you are not or occupy a position to which you are not entitled. It is important to know your place and to act accordingly. When this happens, everything will go well.

38 **K'uei** Opposition

You are facing major opposition, particularly in a relationship, and feel as though you are engaged in an uphill struggle. Do not assume that all paths are blocked and that progress is impossible simply because you cannot make great strides forward. Small steps will eventually enable you to overcome the present situation and resolve it.

39 **Chien** Obstacles

You are about to encounter a major obstacle. It will be best to retreat from it and not continue on your current path. Plot your course carefully and think through your strategy in advance. Be firm and steadfast, and act honourably. Someone will give you excellent advice.

40 **Hsieh** Liberation

If you want to avoid danger you should act quickly. Tie up any loose ends that might otherwise lead to trouble. This is not a good time to introduce new plans and ventures – concentrate on existing arrangements. Do not change anything simply for the sake of it because familiarity breeds content now.

41 **Sun** Decrease

Any form of excess needs to be corrected. This is a good opportunity to make conscious reductions in various areas of your life. Even small reductions will bring you success if you make them in good faith and with sincerity. If you are asked to make a sacrifice it would be better to make a small one willingly than to make a large one grudgingly .

42 **I** Increase

Everything is going well and all your ventures will be successful. Provided you are willing to make progress without injuring anyone, you will enjoy tremendous results and a rise in your fortunes. It is a good time for travel. Be generous with your possessions and blessings.

43 **Kuai** Breakthrough

If you want to succeed you must be earnest and sincere. You should also be conscious of any peril that you will place yourself in, perhaps through people in competition with you. You must focus on the truth, and this may involve denouncing someone who has done wrong. Be cautious when doing this.

44 **Kou** Encounters

This is not a good time to enter into any form of partnership with someone you have only recently met. They are not the person you imagine them to be and they are weaker and less able than you think. They will have a weakening effect on you. It is very important to act in the correct way and to do what you know to be right.

45 **Ts'ui** Gathering Together

This is a very good time to gather together with others, such as your family, friends or colleagues. It will lead to prosperity and success, provided you behave properly and show respect to everyone, especially those who have seniority or authority. Nevertheless, things may not work out in precisely the way you expect.

46 **Shêng** Moving Upwards

Success is on the way. Your stock is rising and you are making excellent progress. Do not be worried if you are about to attend an important interview or meeting because everything will go well and you will have cause to celebrate. You might receive promotion or be placed in a position of power because you can combine determination and modesty.

47 **K'un** Exhaustion

You currently feel that your options are limited but do not give up hope. There is no point in wasting your energy in arguments or pleading words because they will work against you. Instead, accepting the current situation while remaining optimistic and keeping your integrity will lead to eventual success.

48 **Ching** The Well

A town's well cannot be moved, nor can it be depleted by the people who draw their water from it. Even when these people die, the well remains the same. However, problems arise if the rope is too short for the well or the water jug breaks. Make sure you are not being too ambitious or greedy.

49 **Kô** Revolution

This is a good time to introduce gradual changes, even if you do so in the teeth of opposition. Other people may not accept the necessity for the changes you are planning to make until you have eventually completed them. However, you should not let this deter you because the outcome will be very successful.

50 **Ting** The Cauldron

Something is in the process of change. It is being cooked in the cauldron of life. Instigate this change in ways that will nourish everyone, foster their talents and bring further success. Be prepared to make some sacrifices if necessary and draw on your greatest qualities.

51 **Chên** Shock

What seems at first to be a surprising and shocking upheaval will eventually lead to peace once more. Try to maintain your equilibrium during this turbulent phase, even though you are aware of the dangers that it brings, and do not neglect the joys of life, such as wine, friends and love.

52 **Kên** Stillness

It is important to know when to rest and when to act. Do not rest when you should act, nor act when you should rest. If you remember this, you will have great success. Do your best to keep your thoughts on what is happening in the moment and do not be distracted by memories or anticipation of the future. Remain strong in the here and now.

53 **Chien** Gradual Development

Your progress may be slow but it will be steady. You cannot run before you can walk so do not expect to make more progress than you are ready for. Take things slowly and gradually, but not so slowly that you allow the situation to stagnate. Do things in their correct order.

54 **Kuei Mei** The Marrying Maiden

This hexagram is likened to the unsuccessful marriage of a young girl. Although she anticipates happiness, she is disappointed. It is important to avoid making mistakes at the beginning of an enterprise, and it may be better to abandon it altogether if it contains too many pitfalls.

55 **Fêng** Abundance

Do not feel guilty about your prosperity or your blessings. Be prepared to share your good fortune with others, rather than hoard it or be frightened of losing it. Otherwise, you will spend your life feeling anxious about something that may never happen. Be like the sun at noon and shine your light on everyone around you.

56 **Lü** The Wanderer

If you remain constantly on the move you will not be able to achieve very much. Humility, integrity and perseverance will lead to small successes and good fortune. Any actions that you take at the moment will have tremendous significance, especially if you behave well.

57 **Sun** Gentle Effectiveness

This is a time to concentrate on small improvements rather than revolutionary changes. It may help to seek the advice of someone you respect or who has the necessary experience that you lack. Any minor changes that you make now will work to your advantage.

58 **Tui** Joy

Behaving correctly and being firm will lead to joy, success and progress. Concentrating on what makes you happy will help to offset any problems you are currently facing. Friends in particular are a great blessing to you now so enjoy their company.

59 **Huan** Dispersion

You will enjoy progress and success if you are mindful of what you are trying to achieve and disciplined in making it happen. If you allow your thoughts to be distracted you will not behave in ways that are honourable and correct. Once you allow this to happen, it will be even easier to be distracted in the future.

60 **Chieh** Limitation

You will be successful if you willingly place sensible limitations and restrictions on yourself. These will give you a stable framework within which to operate. However, you will not achieve much at all if you are too strict with yourself or if you allow others to place severe restrictions on you.

61 **Chung Fu** Inner Sincerity

Follow what you believe and have faith in your inner convictions. This will help you to be less self-conscious. Other people will appreciate your obvious sincerity and be influenced by it. Travel will be beneficial and will bring you advantages.

62 **Hsiao Kuo** Staying Small

This is not the time to pursue major ventures and big ambitions or to commit hubris. You will make the greatest progress if you concentrate on small tasks and are content with minor successes. Aiming too high will lead to possible peril and disappointment.

63 **Chi Chi** Completion and the Next Step

Something has been successfully accomplished but small tasks connected with it remain. Your work is not yet over and you must consolidate your current success. Tidy up the loose ends before they start to unravel and lead to disorder and confusion. Take the necessary precautions now.

64 **Wei Chi** Before Completion

You have yet to complete something. It began well but is in danger of ending in disarray or confusion because of your complacency about your imminent success. Do not take thoughtless risks that will jeopardize the eventual outcome. Complete tasks in their proper order and at the right time.

palmistry

Our hands do not lie. We might have facelifts to disguise our age but we can do nothing about the wear and tear on our hands. We can put on a show of bravado but our nervous hand movements will give us away. And we can protest that we have a particular set of character traits but our hands may tell a different story.

If you are an avid student of human nature, palmistry is an essential tool. Even a cursory knowledge of the principles of palmistry will help you to avoid buying used cars from people who would sell their own grandmother if they could get the asking price. Palmistry will also sound a warning if you are falling in love with someone fickle; later on, when nursing your broken heart, at least you will have the satisfaction of knowing that your palmistry skills are reliable even if your instincts for self-preservation could do with a refresher course.

The shape and texture of our hands, as well as the bumps and lines that appear on them, describe our character. Palmistry can also reveal our future through the lines on our palms. Skilled practitioners of medical palmistry can diagnose illnesses in a remarkable amount of detail, although such techniques are beyond the scope of this book.

Once you become interested in palmistry, you will find continual opportunities to test your knowledge. When watching a politician on television, study his or her hands. Do you now trust this person? Notice the hands of the person sitting next to you on the bus or train. And look at the hands of your loved ones – they may help you to understand them better.

giving a reading

The best way to start studying palmistry is to look at your own hands. What do they tell you about your life and your personality? You may be thrilled by some discoveries and less pleased about others. Remember, we all have our faults. You might also be perplexed to find that your hand contains contradictions. However, when you think about this you will realize that we are all a mass of contradictions and your hands simply reflect this.

It is vital to read palms in a good light. If you don't have a strong source of natural light, position an artificial lamp over the hands and make sure that there are no shadows falling on them, causing visual distortions. Use a magnifying glass if your eyes are poor, or if you are looking at a hand with a complex web of fine lines.

A professional palmist usually sits opposite the client, with the client's hands resting on the table between them. You may prefer a different arrangement, but it is important to make sure that both you and the other person feel comfortable. It can be tiring holding your outstretched hands in the air for an extended period!

Whether you are giving someone else a reading or reading your own hands, always remember to tone down any bad news or strongly subjective interpretations. Some palmistry books, especially those published a long time ago, seem to delight in doom-laden interpretations calculated to strike terror into one's heart. According to these books, virtually every line and mark on your hand predicts death by drowning, incurable mental illness or total bankruptcy. They can also be very scathing about perfectly normal human foibles, so try not to get drawn into being a holier-than-thou palmist who looks down on the rest of humanity from a lofty perch on Mount Olympus.

There are so many elements to study in a palmistry reading that it is helpful to conduct it in a particular order. It may be tempting to dispense with the mundane stuff and immediately get involved with the intricacies of the lines, but this can mean that you forget to mention some essential pieces of information. Start with the broad brush strokes, studying the shape and texture of the hands, and end with the details, indicated by the lines. This will give your reading more authority and also give you time to get used to the person's hands. While you are studying their hands, take note of what your intuition is telling you, as this may give you useful information. If you are very sensitive, you will also gain insight into this person from their energy field, even if you are not conscious that this is happening.

While looking at the person's hands, it helps to counter any embarrassing silences if you can tell them what you see. Sometimes, of course, this requires tact! If someone's fingernails are broken and embedded with dirt, and their hands are covered with scars from rose thorns, you do not have to be Sherlock Holmes to realize that they are probably a keen gardener. Try to blend this with other information from their hands. For instance, if their hands show that they are highly strung and tend to worry, you can say that their love of gardening helps them to relax and is a way for them to ground themselves. But the dirt under their fingernails may indicate something else. A lack of personal vanity, perhaps? Or that they left home in a hurry? Or perhaps that they are not interested in presenting a conventional appearance?

Before you begin a reading, ask the person if they are right- or left-handed. You always read the hand that they write with, then compare your observations with the other hand. The hand with which we write describes the situations and events that take place in our lives – it shows what happens to us. The other hand describes our potential and the shadow side of our personality. For instance, if you read the palm of someone whose non-writing hand indicates a lot more creativity than they express in their daily life, they are holding themselves back in some way.

You must also ask the person how old they are. If they are shy about revealing their venerable age, persuade them to give you a rough indication, such as being in their fifties. You need this information if you want to predict the person's future – there is no point in telling someone that they will have a radical career change at the age of forty if they are actually fifty-five and the incident is long past.

Finally, if you become interested in palmistry you will be fascinated to watch the lines on your hand gradually changing over the years. You might wish to photocopy your palms, or take prints of them at regular intervals, in order to keep track of any changes. Although the main lines on your hand will not change shape, they can become stronger or fainter, and develop forks, chains and other markings.

the four shapes of the hand

There are several complicated ways of categorizing and analysing the shape of the hand, but one of the easiest was developed by the British palmist Fred Gettings. It divides the hand into four types, each linked with an astrological element – Fire, Earth, Air or Water. The element that rules your hands may not be the element that rules your Sun sign, so do not worry if they do not match.

This system classifies palms as square or long, and fingers as short or long. The combination of the shape of the palm and the length of the fingers describes the overall shape of the hand. This is not an exact science, so you must be adaptable. If the shape of a palm is not immediately obvious, measure it from the base of the middle finger to the base of the palm, and then from side to side. To check the length of the fingers, align the base of the middle finger with the base of the opposite palm. If the finger is at least three-quarters the length of the palm, the fingers are considered to be long.

the fire hand

This hand has a combination of a long palm and short fingers. As well as the major lines, it has many clearly delineated minor lines. It feels warm and dry to the touch. Someone with a Fire hand is enthusiastic and energetic. They like to get as much out of life as possible, and are happier as leaders rather than followers. They enjoy being the centre of attention, and may unconsciously create a drama whenever life threatens to become boring.

the earth hand

With its short palm and short fingers, this is the hand of someone who is very practical and capable. The skin is often coarse and the hand feels hard. They have few minor lines on their hand, as if these are fripperies that they can do without. This is the essence of the owner of an Earth hand – they are honest to the point of being blunt, and do not like wasting time. They are traditional and conventional, have a no-nonsense quality, and can struggle to adapt to change. They may also be sceptical about having their palm read!

the air hand

This hand has a square palm and long fingers. The lines may be thin but are strongly marked. The skin is dry and soft. This person is intelligent and analytical. They place great importance on knowledge and like to retain independence even when in a committed relationship. As born communicators, their career may reflect this. The size and shape of their Mercury finger, plus the length and quality of their head line, will tell you more about their intelligence and ability to communicate.

the water hand

There is often a delicate, aesthetic look to this hand with its long palm and long fingers. It can have many minor, finely marked lines that resemble a spider's web running across the hand. The major lines may look similarly fragile because they are chained, or made up of tiny links. The skin is soft and damp. This person is highly sensitive, intuitive, easily influenced by other people and their surroundings, and often drawn to an artistic or contemplative career. Sometimes they have slightly delicate health or are adversely affected by unpleasant situations.

the elements of the hand

the thumb

This will tell you a tremendous amount about someone. Some palmists believe it is the single most important element of a hand, partly because it reveals so much information about the personality and partly because it is an essential component of any efficient hand.

When you begin to study palmistry, you will realize that hands with weak or small thumbs look unfinished and unbalanced. And indeed, a weak thumb denotes someone who lacks a strong personality and may seem wishy-washy. They may also have a weak character. Equally, a strong thumb shows a strong character. When you see a thumb that dominates the hand, especially if it looks coarse, it shows someone with a domineering personality.

To establish the length of the thumb, examine its position on the hand. What appears to be a short thumb may actually be a long thumb set far down the hand towards the wrist, or the converse may apply. The average thumb begins halfway down the hand. This shows someone with a moderate, well-balanced ego. A thumb set high on the hand, near the index or Jupiter finger, indicates someone who is very full of themselves and has an over-developed ego. A thumb set low on the hand shows someone who is practical but perhaps not very intellectual. They may also have little ego.

An average thumb is roughly the same length as the little or Mercury finger. People with this kind of thumb are sensitive to other people's needs while being able to speak up for themselves when necessary. A long thumb belongs to someone who has a strong character. If the thumb is also broad, it shows someone who is ambitious and determined to achieve their objectives. A long but narrow thumb indicates someone whose ambitions may not be realized because they lack the required motivation.

Someone with a short thumb has a weak character. They are compliant to the point of lacking direction, and may be unrealistic about life. If the thumb is also narrow, this person may not achieve much in worldly terms and may seem to coast along aimlessly. The situation is slightly improved with a short but broad thumb – this person has energy but lacks the drive to channel it in useful directions. If the thumb is small to the point of looking weak, it shows someone who is equally weak. They lack personality and sparkle, and are always trailing in the wake of others.

Unlike the fingers, the thumb has two phalanges or segments. The top segment rules will and the lower one rules logic. Check the thumb to see which segment is longer and therefore whether the person's heart rules their head or vice versa. A longer second segment shows someone who relies on logic. The longer this segment, the more logical the person. If the upper segment is so broad and bulky that the thumb looks top-heavy, the person is stubborn to the point of wilfulness and is also a bully. They may not care how they get results, as long as they get them. When you see this top phalange on a short thumb, you may be dealing with someone who is violent or has a powerful temper.

Violence is also shown by a very bulbous top segment when viewed from the side. A less exaggerated curve shows someone who is outspoken and can appear rude. No curve at all indicates someone who is very sensitive and does not like upsetting others.

The flexibility of the thumb will tell you a lot about the way the person's mind works. The more flexible the top segment, the greater the mental flexibility. So a rigid thumb shows someone who is resistant to change, but who is reliable. A thumb that bends over slightly indicates someone who can appreciate more than one point of view, and who may change their own mind quite often. When the thumb bends a long way, it shows someone who often bends the truth to suit the situation.

the fingers

These will tell you an enormous amount about your personality. You might imagine that everyone's fingers are the same length and shape, but once you have started studying palms you will be astonished by the variety of fingers you come across.

The four fingers are named after four Roman gods. The index finger is named after Jupiter, the middle finger after Saturn, the ring finger after Apollo and the little finger after Mercury. If you have some astrological knowledge, you will find many similarities between the meanings of these fingers and the planets whose names they bear.

In most hands, the Saturn finger is the longest, followed by the Jupiter finger, the Apollo finger and lastly the Mercury finger. A normal-sized Saturn finger is about three-quarters the length of the palm. A normal Jupiter finger reaches the middle of the top phalange of the normal Saturn finger. The Apollo finger is normally slightly shorter than Jupiter. A normal Mercury finger reaches the top joint of the normal Apollo finger. When studying the length of the fingers, remember that some of the fingers may start from lower down on the palm. For instance, what seems at first to be a small index finger may be much longer because of its low position on the palm.

the Jupiter finger

The index finger describes the amount of pride someone has. The longer the finger, the prouder the person. With pride can come arrogance, so this may be someone who believes they are always right. They are a good leader, may be wilful and may crave power.

A short Jupiter finger indicates someone who prefers to follow in the wake of others. They can be very shy and may be reluctant to reach independent decisions for fear of losing face. An average-sized Jupiter finger shows a healthy amount of self-confidence. Someone who wears a ring on this finger is trying to bolster their self-confidence and appear more powerful than they feel. This is especially true if the finger is short. If it is long, the person has a high opinion of themselves.

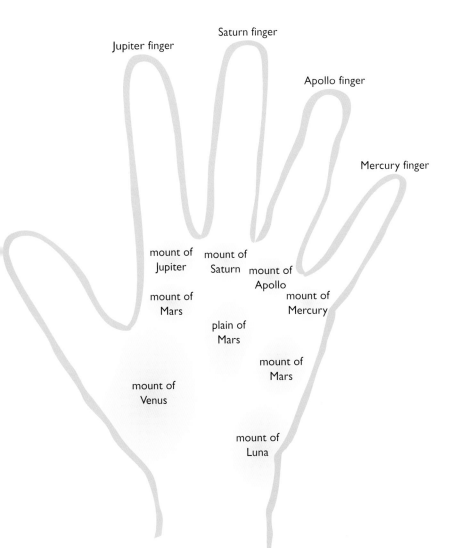

Jupiter finger

Saturn finger

Apollo finger

Mercury finger

mount of Jupiter

mount of Saturn

mount of Apollo

mount of Mars

mount of Mercury

plain of Mars

mount of Mars

mount of Venus

mount of Luna

the Saturn finger

This is the middle finger. It rules responsibility and duty, so a long
Saturn finger indicates someone who is reliable. They are solid
and dependable, and may take a slightly gloomy view of life. They
may also have a tendency to shoulder a lot of burdens by taking
on more than their fair share of responsibility. If this is the most
prominent finger on the hand, the person may be prone to
depression and will take life very seriously.

A short Saturn finger indicates someone who shies away
from responsibility. Rather than think things through in the
manner of someone with a long Saturn finger, they will rush to
hasty conclusions and hope for the best. A very short Saturn
finger can show an almost pathological inability to deal with
commitment. This person is unlikely to be married!

If someone wears a ring on this finger they are trying to boost their sense of security. This may be to help them through a difficult phase, but you will know more by studying the length of this finger.

the Apollo finger

The ring finger shows someone's creative abilities and emotions. An average length of finger shows a moderately artistic person with well-balanced emotions. A long Apollo finger indicates someone who is no stranger to intense emotions and who often expresses them in fulsome ways. They may even seem slightly larger than life. They are also very creative. The rest of their hand, including its shape, will contain clues about how they channel their creativity.

A short Apollo finger shows someone who struggles to express their emotions – they may seem closed off from the rest of the world in some way. They will also find it hard to tolerate other people's emotional needs. They can seem rather listless and may have a floppy handshake. This is the finger on which most people in the West wear their engagement and/or wedding ring. If the person is not married or in a committed relationship, yet wears a ring on the Apollo finger of their left hand, ask yourself why. Perhaps they are subtly rejecting possible partners?

the Mercury finger

The length of this finger can be misleading! Very often what seems to be a short Mercury finger is actually a long finger set far down on the hand. Move the hand so that the bases of the fingers are level, then measure the Mercury against the Apollo finger. This will tell you whether it is really as short as you imagined. A normal Mercury finger reaches the top joint of the Apollo.

As its name suggests, the Mercury finger rules communication. An average Mercury finger shows someone who has few problems when communicating with others. A long one indicates someone who excels at communicating and may even make their living from it. They are probably chatty and certainly lively. They may also have above-average intelligence, even if they do not give themselves credit for this (lack of self-esteem may be shown in other areas of their hand).

When someone has a short Mercury finger they find it difficult to make contact with others. There are frequent misunderstandings, making them irritable and frustrated. There may also be something childlike about them, possibly their voice or their manner of speaking.

Another indication of character is the shape of the Mercury finger. If it is straight, the person is honest. A crooked Mercury finger suggests someone who at best often exaggerates and at worst may tell lies. Of course, this does not apply to fingers that have become bent through illness or accidents. This tendency to distort the truth is confirmed if the tops of the thumbs bend forwards.

If this finger seems to stand apart from the rest of the hand, it shows a very independent spirit. This person may have something special to communicate to the world. If they naturally hold their finger away from the Apollo finger, they have a strong need to be solitary and will suffer when they do not have enough time to themselves.

When someone wears a ring on this finger they are trying to boost their communication skills. If their finger suggests they are dishonest, the presence of a ring on this finger will emphasize this trait.

the mounts

A mount is the small fleshy pad that appears on the palm at the base of each finger. Not every finger has its own mount – sometimes the mount will sit between two of the fingers. Mounts are also found elsewhere on the palm.

the mount of Jupiter

This is found at the base of the index, or Jupiter, finger. A small mount shows a lack of confidence. The bigger the mount, the more pronounced the person's ambition and desire for success. You will be able to tell if such ambitions will ever be realized by looking for a strong life line. However, if the life line is weak, the person's dreams will all be pie in the sky.

the mount of Saturn

This mount sits at the base of the middle, or Saturn, finger. The stronger the mount, the more serious and conservative the person. If it is very large, the person may be pessimistic and gloomy. If the mount does not exist this denotes someone who takes life as it comes. However, before you reach this conclusion, check that the mount has not merged with either the Jupiter or Apollo mount. A Jupiter/Saturn mount indicates ambition and a Jupiter/Apollo mount shows artistry.

the mount of Apollo

This is found at the base of the ring, or Apollo, finger. A well-shaped mount indicates creativity, generosity and a love of beauty. A very large mount shows someone who enjoys being the centre of attention. This mount may have merged with the Saturn mount.

the mount of Mercury

This mount sits at the base of the little, or Mercury, finger. It amplifies the characteristics shown on the rest of the hand, especially the head line. A well-shaped mount on a positive hand with a strong head line denotes a lively wit and a quick mind. However, if the head line is weak and the hand is negative, this mount indicates someone who can be unreliable, untrustworthy and sarcastic.

the mount of Mars

You will find two of these on the hand – one sits below the mount of Jupiter and the other below the mount of Mercury. They both denote courage. An absence of either mount indicates a lack of the characteristic that its presence bestows.

Physical courage is shown by the mount below the mount of Jupiter. This person is happy to back their words with action. If the mount is very large they are dogmatic and take foolish risks. Moral courage is indicated by the mount below the mount of Mercury. A well-developed mount shows someone with willpower and the courage of their convictions. A very large mount shows someone who is evangelical about their beliefs to the point of insensitivity.

the plain of Mars

Strictly speaking, this is not a mount. It is found in the centre of the palm, surrounded by the other mounts. It is a good indicator of self-confidence. The more you can feel the person's bones and tendons through the plain of Mars, the greater their lack of confidence. A firm and elastic plain indicates someone with confidence. A full, fleshy plain of Mars shows someone who is very full of themselves and likes the sound of their own voice.

the mount of Luna

You will find this mount on the outer edge of the hand, below the mount of Mars and above the wrist. A flat mount shows someone who is realistic and has their feet on the ground. A well-developed mount indicates someone who is artistic, imaginative and who may be telepathic. A pronounced mount indicates someone who is otherworldly and a dreamer. If their Mercury finger and head line concur, they have a tenuous grasp of reality and may lead a Walter Mitty existence.

the mount of Venus

This mount is the muscle at the base of the thumb, covering what is actually the third phalange of the thumb. It shows the level of vitality and enthusiasm for life. The more pronounced the mount, the more the person enjoys life. They are probably artistic, have a high sex drive and plenty of energy. A flabby or flat mount shows someone who is listless and lethargic, with a low sex drive.

the four major lines

When you tell someone you are a palmist, probably the first thing they will do is hold out their palm and ask about the length of their life line. You will doubtless be equally curious about your own lifespan, wondering what the lines on your hand have to say.

Once you start studying palms, after scrutinizing your own, you will soon realize that there is almost no limit to the differences in the lines on people's palms. You will encounter some hands where there are only the basic lines, clearly defined, with no subsidiary lines. Other hands will be a network of fine lines, apparently heading in every direction, which intersect the main lines. You will also find hands where the lines merge together, making it very difficult to know where one ends and the next one starts.

The same rules apply to lines as they do to the fingers and mounts on the hand. The stronger the line, the stronger the characteristics with which it is associated. In other words, the energies denoted by that line are flowing well within the person. If you find a weak line, the energies of that line are not being fully expressed. Interruptions to a line, such as breaks, chains or squares, indicate problems in the areas of life denoted by that line. However, with practice you will come to realize that most of us have such marks on the lines of our hands, and that very few people go through life unscathed by problems. You must also learn to differentiate between the problems experienced by people who are very sensitive and those who are more robust. The very sensitive may react more strongly to situations that robust people can shrug off easily. Different people may react very differently to the same situation.

the life line

This is one of the two lines that everyone wants to know about. As its name suggests, it describes the path that someone's life takes, and any major illnesses and incidents are clearly shown. The life line starts on the edge of the palm at some point between the thumb and the Jupiter finger and runs around the mount of Venus, finishing somewhere near the wrist.

There is a simplistic belief that the longer the line, the longer the life. However, this is not necessarily true. It is only in horror films that a palmist looks at someone's life line and tells them they should already be dead. The quality of the line is as important an indicator of longevity as the length of the line, and even then there may be mitigating factors elsewhere on the palm. It is best to avoid this subject and not pronounce on anyone's expected lifespan.

Nevertheless, the life line will tell you a lot about someone's health. Generally speaking, the stronger and more clearly marked the life line, the better the person's health. However, a very red life line can indicate health problems. If the life line is feathery, poorly marked and pale, encourage the person to take better care of themselves.

Look for breaks in the line or small lines that run across it. These show illnesses and periods of general ill health. If there are breaks in the line, look for small lines that connect the two halves of the line. These will show that the person is able to survive the experience. If you cannot see any links between the broken lines at all, the incident described will mark the definite demarcation between the end of one chapter in the person's life and the start of the next. If the break appears in both hands, the incident it describes will have a profound effect. If it appears only in one hand, the incident will not have such a strong impact. If the life line becomes stronger or more curved after the break, the person's life will become more enjoyable and fulfilling after the incident. If the life line becomes weaker or straighter, the person's life will not be as satisfying and happy as it was before the incident.

If someone has a guardian angel, the life line is where you will find it. Look for a subsidiary line, between the mount of Venus and the life line, that runs beside the line for part or all of its length. This shows that the person is being given protection during the phase shown by the line, whether from an unseen guardian angel or through a fellow human. Most people are delighted to be told this.

The shape of the line will tell you a great deal. The more generous the curve of the life line, the greater the energy and zest of the person. If the line is barely curved, the person is shy, introverted and self-contained. They find it hard to deal with other people and may also be scared of living life to the full. A straight line that cuts through the mount of Venus shows someone who is self-centred, ungenerous and negative.

Look to see where the life line starts. If it begins on the mount of Jupiter, the person has been ambitious since childhood. If it starts lower down the hand, near the thumb, they are not very imaginative. If it is joined to the head line, the person struggles to make decisions. This may because they are heavily influenced by other people, such as their family. If there is a small gap between the start of the head and life lines, the person has a normal level of independence. The wider the gap between the two lines, the more independent the person.

Study the end of the life line, since this will describe the end of the person's life. However, avoid making definite pronouncements that might worry the person unduly. If the line comes to a sudden stop, the person will carry on strong until they die. If the line peters out, the person will become weaker as they get older. When it curves around the mount of Venus, it shows a love of home and home comforts. When it curves towards the mount of Luna, it shows a love of travel. If there is a fork, look for the strongest line because this will show whether travel wins over love of home, or vice versa.

the fate line

Despite its imposing name, it is sometimes difficult to locate this line on the hand. When it is present, it runs up the centre of the hand from the base of the palm to the mount of Saturn. Very often it will appear strongly on one hand and much more

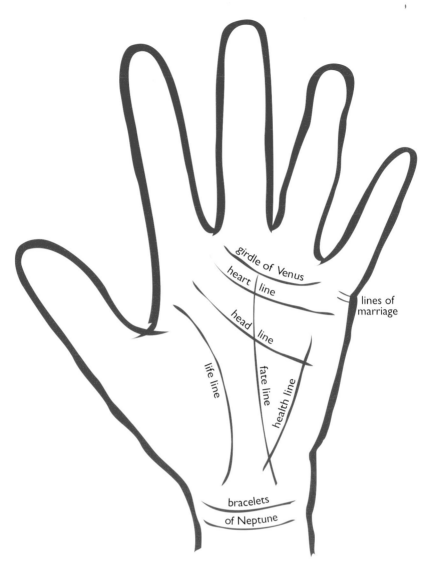

Image labels: girdle of Venus, heart line, head line, lines of marriage, life line, fate line, health line, bracelets of Neptune

sketchily on the other. Sometimes, it is absent on both hands, which means the person dislikes routine and prefers to let life happen without much forward planning. The lack of a fate line does not mean the lack of a fate! A strong line indicates someone who is reliable, practical and good at planning.

When there is a fate line on the person's writing hand but not on the other hand, they channel a lot of effort into achieving their aims. When the line only exists on the non-writing hand, the person is full of dreams and plans that never see the light of day.

One of the reasons it can be difficult to locate the fate line on a hand is because it can start and end in several different places. The higher up the hand the fate line starts, the older the person is before they discover their path in life. If it starts low down on the hand, near the wrist, the person knew their own mind and what they wanted to do with their life from an early age. If it starts on the mount of Luna, the person has expressed their creativity and ambitions from an early age. If it starts on the mount of Venus, within the life line, the person will obey their family's wishes about the direction of their life until the point where the line moves away from the life line on to the plain of Mars.

Now look to see where the line ends. If it runs from the wrist to a mount, that mount will describe the area of life in which the person is successful. If it runs through the mount of Saturn and touches the Saturn finger, the person will continue to work long after their contemporaries have retired. If the line finishes at the heart line, their ambitions will falter because of an emotional disappointment. If it finishes at the head line, their ambitions will falter because of poor judgement. Look also to see if any lines run from the fate line to the mount of Jupiter. These are a good indicator of success. Success and power are assured if the fate line itself ends on the mount of Jupiter.

As a simple rule, the more breaks in someone's fate line, the more changes they will experience in their career and life. If the breaks overlap, the person will be preparing for the next chapter in their life while still being involved in the previous one, even if they are not aware of it at the time. Distinct breaks with no overlaps show sudden endings and beginnings. A very flimsy line means the person fritters away their energy and does not achieve very much.

the heart line

In addition to the life line, this is the line that most people want to know about! As its name implies, it describes the quality of our emotional life and our attitude to relationships. It begins from some point under the mount of Mercury and ends around the mounts of Saturn or Jupiter.

Sometimes, you will be mystified because there is only one line running across the hand. This is called the simian line and is actually a combined heart and head line. As you would expect, the owner of this hand finds it impossible to separate their emotions from their reasoning. They struggle to be objective because there is no division between their thoughts and feelings.

The condition of the line will tell you a lot about the person's relationships. A very clear and strongly marked line, with few subsidiary lines, shows someone who is constant in their affections but rather self-centred. They are not very sensitive to other people's moods and needs. A weak, feathery line shows someone who is not very faithful and who may struggle to maintain successful relationships. However, it is important to consider the shape of the line before reaching any definite conclusions. The more curved the line, the more sensitive the person is towards other people. The straighter the line, the less concerned they are about satisfying the needs of others. The longer the line, the greater the range of the person's emotions. A very short line therefore indicates someone whose emotions are limited. A very long line shows someone whose life is ruled by their emotions.

The heart line always starts under the mount of Mercury. However, it can end in a variety of places. If it ends on the mount of Saturn, it denotes someone who takes their emotional life very seriously. They are passionate and will sometimes allow their feelings to run away with them. This will be emphasized if the mount of Venus is large and has a good colour.

If the line ends between the Jupiter and Saturn fingers, the person has well-balanced emotions. They are emotional without allowing themselves to get out of control. The person whose heart line ends on the mount of Jupiter is an emotional idealist. They always think the best of their loved ones and are inevitably hurt when their ideals are shattered. Nevertheless, they are faithful and loyal. When the line ends on the side of the palm, the person experiences a wide variety of emotions, including possessiveness and jealousy.

If the heart line ends in a fork, their emotions will be a blend of the characteristics shown by the different endings. One fork may be stronger than the others, in which case this is the characteristic that will predominate. However, try to differentiate between forks running from the heart line and lines that are an extension of the fate line. Sometimes it is difficult to tell the difference, in which case you should rely on your intuition and what the rest of the hand is telling you.

The higher the heart line sits on the hand, the sunnier the person's disposition and the more successful their relationships. Equally, the lower the heart line, the more difficult their relationships can be. As you would imagine, breaks in the heart line indicate interruptions in the person's relationships. The size of the break, and any corresponding breaks in the fate or life lines, will show the level of impact this incident had on the person.

the head line

You will find this line under the heart line, running across the plain of Mars. It starts near the life line and ends somewhere under the Mercury finger. It shows the way someone's mind works and their level of intellect.

The stronger the head line, the more pronounced the person's mental abilities. A clear-cut, well-marked line that runs across the palm shows someone who knows their own mind. They are not easily swayed by argument, which means they have the courage of their convictions but can be stubborn and dogmatic. The lighter and more feathery the head line, the more the person struggles to keep control of their thoughts. Their opinions may vacillate and they may not have much common sense. The length of the line will emphasize or mitigate these findings. The shorter the line, the more hasty the person. A long line shows someone who spends a lot of time wrapped in thought and can sometimes get bogged down in their ideas.

The line can start in one of three places – underneath the life line, joined to the start of the life line or on the mount of Jupiter. If the line starts beneath the life line, the person is very influenced by other people's opinions. They are shy, lack self-confidence and are indecisive because they always want to do the right thing and not upset anyone. When the head and life lines begin together, the person is heavily influenced by the demands and opinions of their family. The longer the two lines are joined together, the longer the family's influence will be felt. If the head line starts on the mount of Jupiter, the person is confident and enjoys a certain amount of independence.

You will also learn a lot from seeing where the head line ends. It can run down to the mount of Luna, end in a fork or curve up towards one of the fingers. If it ends near the mount of Luna, this shows a powerful and fertile imagination but a possible tendency to be depressive. When the head line ends in a fork, this is known as the writer's fork. As its name suggests, it is the classic sign of a writer. A head line that curves up towards one of the fingers is influenced by the area of life ruled by that finger. So a line that curves up towards the Apollo finger describes someone who is very creative. If the line curves up towards the Mercury finger, the person is a born communicator.

Breaks in the head line indicate times when the person has changed their mind about something. If the life or heart lines also show breaks that fit the same time scale, you can safely assume that the person experienced a complete turning point in their life at this point.

the minor lines

There are many minor, supplementary lines on the hand, but here are some of the ones you are most likely to come across. You will not always find all these lines on a hand.

the health line

This line is not always present. In fact, it is better not to have it because its absence denotes good health and stamina. It starts at the base of the hand and moves out towards the mount of Mercury. When it is present and rather faint, it shows the person needs to take care of themselves and does not always have the reserves of energy that they would like. When it is present and strongly marked, the person has plenty of energy.

the girdle of Venus

This line sits between the heart line and the base of the fingers. It runs from some point around the mounts of Jupiter and Saturn to the mounts of Apollo and Mercury. It shows a flirtatious disposition and an ability to get on well with others. This person is sensitive and has a passionate nature that can extend beyond their relationships to other areas of their life, such as their career.

the bracelets of Neptune

You will find these lines curved around the base of the wrist, as their name suggests. Tradition says they indicate luck, especially for people who have more than the usual two lines. If the bracelets are chained, they show a lack of stamina.

the lines of marriage

These short, horizontal lines sit on the side of the palm between the heart line and the base of the Mercury finger. Old palmistry books described them as lines of marriage because, at the time, marriage was the social norm. Today, these lines are taken to indicate the most important relationships in a person's life. The stronger the line, the more important the relationship.

timing events

This is one of the most difficult aspects of palmistry to master. In theory, you mentally divide each line into segments that allow you to judge roughly when events will take place. For instance, a break in the middle of the life line will occur roughly in the middle of that person's life. In practice, this is not as easy as it sounds. Everyone's hands are different, with lines of differing lengths. You also have to decide on an average lifespan and divide the lines up accordingly. Seventy-five is a reasonable figure, although, of course, you will have to revise your views if the person concerned is older than this. It is also important to remember the points at which the lines begin, so that you can see which part of each line relates to the early life:

- the life line begins at the top of the thumb
- the fate line begins at the base of the wrist
- the heart line begins at the outer edge of the palm
- the head line begins near the top of the thumb

When timing events on a line, divide it into four so you have a rough idea of which events happened in the late teens, the late thirties and the early fifties. It will help considerably if you have some sort of yardstick to go by. For instance, if there is a break in the life line that shows changes during the person's childhood, ask them at what age these events took place. This will give you something to work from. If you are trying to time events on a line that is unusually short, imagine that the line begins or ends in the normal place and divide it up accordingly.

One of the questions you will hear most often is whether the person will have any more important relationships in their life. The marriage lines begin from the heart line, so mentally quarter the section of hand between the heart line and the base of the Mercury finger, then work out the position of the marriage lines accordingly.

numerology

Numerology is an ancient art based on numbers. Pythagoras, the Greek mathematician, was the instigator of the numerology we practise today. He believed that numbers rule everything in the world and that once we discover the numerical value of something we can define it accordingly.

Numerology is a marvellous tool for discovering the hidden meanings of your name and date of birth, which give your personality and destiny numbers respectively. You can also use it to gain more insight into the people you know. If you wish, you can use numerology to select the name of your baby, house, company, car or anything else that is of value to you. An example of how to use numerology to choose your baby's name is given at the end of the chapter.

Ideally, an individual's destiny and personality numbers should both be odd or even, to allow the energies to flow more harmoniously. Odd numbers are powerful and extrovert, and have traditionally been called masculine. Even numbers are more gentle and introvert, and have traditionally been called feminine. This does not mean that men can only have masculine numbers and women only feminine. However, you will find that men who have only feminine numbers in their name and birth date have much softer personalities than men with nothing but masculine numbers.

Eleven numbers are used in numerology – one to nine, plus eleven and twenty-two. The digits of any other numbers are added together until you arrive at one of the eleven numbers. For example, fifty-seven is reduced by adding five and seven together to make twelve, then adding one and two together to make three. The only two-digit numbers that are not added together are eleven and twenty-two, which are known as master numbers. When you arrive at one of these you do not reduce them any further.

Master numbers are very powerful, purely because they break the usual numerology rule of reducing numbers to single digits. They carry special qualities and often denote people who stand out from the crowd in some way, but in themselves are no 'better' or 'worse' than any other number.

In this chapter you will learn how to discover the following numbers:

• Your destiny number, from your date of birth
• Your personality number, from your name
• Your expression number, from the consonants in your name
• Your heart number, from the vowels in your name

calculating your destiny number

This number, derived from your date of birth, has special significance because it cannot be changed legally. It therefore describes the lessons you will learn throughout your life. This is a very simple number to calculate – all you do is add up the numbers in your birth date until you reach one of the eleven numbers.

This is how you do it, using Greta Garbo as an example. She was born on 18 September 1905. Write this down in numerical form, translating the month of the year into its numerical equivalent – January is one, December is twelve. Ignore any noughts.

$$1 + 8 + 9 + 1 + 9 + 5 = 33$$
$$3 + 3 = 6$$

Greta Garbo's destiny number is therefore six. If she had used an assumed birth date, perhaps shaving a few years off her real age, you would calculate this as well, because it would tell you how she wanted to be seen by others.

calculating your personality, expression and heart numbers

This number is derived from the letters in the name by which you are usually known. If you have a middle name but never use it in your ordinary activities, do not include it. If you have a nickname, or you are known by a contraction of your real name (such as Mike instead of Michael), use this. You can always calculate your personality number using your original name and compare it with the personality number of your ordinary name. It is especially interesting to do this with people who use pseudonyms or stage names.

First, you need to convert the letters in your name into numbers, using the table on the next page:

1	2	3	4	5	6	7	8	9
A	B	C	D	E	F	G	H	I
J	K	L	M	N	O	P	Q	R
S	T	U	V	W	X	Y	Z	

When working out the personality number of a name with no vowels but containing a Y, always count the Y as a vowel. You will understand why this is important in a moment. Some numerologists always count a Y as a vowel, others make their decision according to the way it is pronounced. For instance, they say that Y is a vowel when it is pronounced as such, as in the name Petty, otherwise it is a consonant.

Write down the name, then write the numerical values of the vowels above the name and those of the consonants below the name.

		5		1		1		6
G	R	E	T	A	G	A	R	B	O
7	9		2		7		9	2	

The next step is to add up the numbers representing the vowels:

$$5 + 1 + 1 + 6 = 13$$

Keep reducing the total by adding the numbers together until you arrive at one of the numbers used in numerology:

$$1 + 3 = 4$$

All the vowels in Greta Garbo's name add up to four. This constitutes her heart number, which describes her deepest desires and wishes. Now add up the numbers representing the consonants in her name:

$$7 + 9 + 2 + 7 + 9 + 2 = 36$$
$$3 + 6 = 9$$

So the consonants in Greta Garbo's name add up to nine. This is known as her expression number and it describes the image she presents to the world. The final step is to add together the numbers of the heart (vowels) number and the expression (consonants) number to discover the personality number:

$$4 + 9 = 13$$
$$1 + 3 = 4$$

Greta Garbo's personality number is therefore four. If you wish, you can then calculate the personality, heart and expression numbers for her real name, which was Greta Gustafsson, and see what they say about her. Remember, the numbers of her real name will reveal her true self. Her destiny number is six, which is an even number, so it is in a harmonious relationship with her personality number.

plotting your future with numerology

If you want a successful future, you need to plan accordingly. There is nothing you can do to change your birth date, but you can change your name. If your current name adds up to numbers that do not reflect the future you want for yourself, it may help to alter the spelling of your name slightly, add an initial or even change one of your names in order to arrive at more fortuitous numbers.

You can also use numerology to see what a particular year will bring you. All you need to do is add the year in question to the numbers of your day and month of birth, and then read the interpretation of that particular destiny number. For instance, after Greta Garbo had enjoyed many years of celebrity as a film star she decided to retire in 1941. So what does numerology say about her life that year?

Add together the numbers of the day and month of her birth, plus the numbers for 1941:

$$1 + 8 + 9 + 1 + 9 + 4 + 1 = 33$$
$$3 + 3 = 6$$

So 1941 had the energies of the number six for Garbo. This is the same as her destiny number, so it was a year in which she felt compelled to express her true destiny and to behave in whichever way felt most comfortable. Six is a number associated with a love of home and a resulting tendency to be insular. After Garbo retired, she became famous for her reclusive tendencies and her enjoyment of a contented home life.

You can use this technique to plot which year would be best to concentrate on your career (such as a year that gives a destiny number of eight), your spiritual life (eleven) or travel (five). There are eleven numbers in numerology, so the events in your life conform to an eleven-year cycle. Interestingly, the solar cycle (the activity of the Sun) is roughly eleven years in length, and there may be some correlation between it and the numerological cycle.

This is the first masculine number and also the first prime number, so it is very powerful. It is linked to beginnings. It is linked to the Sun and the sign of Leo.

destiny number This is the number of the innovator and the pioneer. This person does not want to follow in other people's footsteps – they have their own path to take and are natural leaders. They have a strong need to express themselves and to follow their ambitions, regardless of what others think. At best, this makes them strong-minded, but at worst can make them intransigent and obstinate. They are kind and affectionate.

personality number The person with this number has many of the traits of the person above, being a true original and very enterprising. They are also creative and will excel when they use these talents in some way. They do not like being limited or hampered, especially if their destiny number is also one. Variety is the spice of life for them and they soon become bogged down if they lead a predictable or routine existence.

expression number This person is full of confidence and gives the impression of having life all sorted out. They appear to know exactly what they are doing and where they are heading, even if this is far from true. They are born troubleshooters and often find themselves bailing out their many friends. They are very popular, partly because nothing seems to faze them, so they are a comforting presence.

heart number This person sees themselves as innovative, independent and pioneering. They have plenty of confidence and react badly to criticism and advice. In relationships, they find it difficult to show their vulnerable side and can consequently give the impression of being self-sufficient and not very interested in others. They may prefer to be emotionally independent and not involved in a committed relationship.

This is the dual number which rules all opposites. It is associated with harmony, partnership and diplomacy. It is connected with the Moon and the sign of Cancer.

destiny number This person needs to be in a relationship to feel complete. They function best as a team player rather than a solo agent, and are affectionate and kind. They need harmony in their life and will do their utmost to obtain it, sometimes putting themselves at a disadvantage in the process. This can lead to resentment when others take advantage of their easy-going nature. They are prone to being moody because they are scared of being openly confrontational.

personality number Innate tact and diplomacy enable this person to smooth ruffled feathers and maintain harmony. They excel as a mediator, but are not so skilled when it comes to sorting out their own problems. They tend to withdraw from the fray, which is often interpreted as sulking. They are tremendously sensitive and do not like hurting their loved ones. It is tempting for them to hold on to situations, belongings and relationships long after they should have moved on from them.

expression number This person is a perfectionist. They expect the very best from their partners and will soon tick them off if they fail to come up to scratch. They are also very tough and exacting when trying to maintain their own high standards and become annoyed with themselves when they fail. Nevertheless, they are endlessly supportive of partners. They excel at being a tireless background member of a team.

heart number Emotional security and tranquillity are vitally important for this person, who is always thrown by unpleasant scenes and uncomfortable atmospheres. They can give the impression of being very self-assured, but underneath it is a different story because they are so sensitive and vulnerable. They really come into their own in close relationships because they are considerate and supportive.

This number is connected with growth and fresh beginnings, whether physical or mental. It is associated with Jupiter and the sign of Sagittarius.

destiny number Here is someone who excels at relationships, thanks to their cheerful, positive and sunny disposition. They enjoy being part of a family but are not so keen on feeling tied down by responsibility or being expected to carry out lots of tedious tasks. They are very loving although they are not the world's most faithful people. They enjoy travel and challenges.

personality number This person is a born optimist. Their glass is always half full and better times are always just around the corner. This positive attitude seems to work, because they are successful and may have a burgeoning career that keeps them very busy. They excel in any job that involves communicating with others and may become well known in their field as a result. They take care with their appearance, but are not slavish about following fashion. They need plenty of variety in their life, otherwise they soon become bored and fed up.

expression number This person is full of confidence and great fun to be around. It is difficult to ignore them because they are often the main focus of attention, and for all the right reasons. Here is an instinctive performer who knows exactly how to command an audience. They seem to be effortlessly confident and amusing. Nevertheless, they are uncomfortable when they are out of the limelight for long.

heart number Good company and a born optimist, this person is deservedly popular. They are an excellent friend and partner because they are genuinely supportive of loved ones and want them to do well. They are generous with their congratulations when people succeed, and full of encouragement when they encounter setbacks. Although they have a marvellous sense of humour and seem to be the life and soul of the party, they may be hiding a very vulnerable side that longs for acceptance and love.

Four is associated with stability, tradition and structure, and connected with Saturn and the sign of Capricorn.

destiny number Here is someone with tremendous potential, ability and sticking power. They will doggedly pursue an ambition until they have achieved it, sometimes to the cost of other areas of their life. For instance, their relationships may suffer because of the emphasis they place on work and responsibility. Although they are capable of enjoying themselves, they can be slightly puritanical about having too much hedonistic fun. They often have to overcome problems or limitations early in life. Their home is very important to them.

personality number This person needs to feel their life has a solid structure, otherwise they become anxious and full of trepidation. They have a tendency to get bogged down in routine because they are wary of being too spontaneous. They excel at being practical and organized, and only feel truly comfortable when everything is running smoothly, with no room for problems or unexpected events. Yet this is an ideal person to turn to in a crisis because they are level-headed.

expression number This person is probably admired for their resourcefulness, practical abilities and trustworthy character. They are not interested in basking in glory – they are much keener on doing what is expected of them. They are dutiful and responsible, which means others sometimes take them for granted. They are slightly conservative and mistrustful of people who do not conform to their own standards and way of life.

heart number This unassuming person does not like being in the limelight too often. They are much happier working busily behind the scenes, making sure that everything runs smoothly. They like to be considered dependable and reliable. Nature is very important to them and they may harbour a secret wish to spend more time outdoors or even to have a job that brings them into contact with nature.

This is a very creative number. It is also associated with movement, energy and travel. It is linked to Mercury and therefore with the signs of Gemini and Virgo.

destiny number Travel is very enjoyable for this person because they love to keep on the move. They like plenty of variety in their life and can get rather bogged down when things become boring or too predictable. Nevertheless, they need to guard against a tendency to be a mental butterfly who knows a little about a lot but nothing in detail. They are a skilled communicator who is intelligent, charming and quick-witted, and ideally they should put these qualities to good use in their career.

personality number Whenever life threatens to become too staid, routine or dreary, this person will want to shake things up. Sometimes they will introduce change simply for the sake of it, purely to make life more interesting. Their blood quickens at the thought of adventure and they enjoy taking off on holiday. They like to keep one eye on the far horizon, so are always planning things in advance. Sometimes they may be so excited about their future prospects that they neglect to enjoy the present.

expression number If you want to know the latest gossip, ask someone with five as their expression number. They will soon fill you in on anything you have missed! They have plenty of friends, thanks to their intellect, fascinating conversation and wide range of interests. They soon become restless if they feel they are stuck in a routine or have spent too long in one place.

heart number A sense of dissatisfaction and disappointment lurks within this person. They are unhappily aware that life could be so much more exciting, if only they could hit on the secret formula. As a result, they may have a series of broken relationships because no partner ever comes up to scratch. Yet they do become more contented as they get older. Lively and great company, this person makes friends easily, but will soon sever ties with anyone who is not attuned to them mentally.

This number is associated with a love of the family and home, and with service and responsibility. It is connected with Venus and the signs of Taurus and Libra.

destiny number Someone with this number has a strong nesting instinct. A happy home is essential if they are to feel fulfilled. They will channel a lot of energy into looking after their loved ones, sometimes to the point where they neglect their own needs. It is tempting for them to become slightly isolated from the rest of the world because they move in a very small social circle composed of family and close friends. They are affectionate and kind, but can sometimes be possessive and self-centred.

personality number This is someone with an instinctive need to be of service and to help others. They will find many ways to express this, not least through their job, which is probably a vocation. Self-employment comes easily to them, because they are motivated and like to do things well. They take their responsibilities seriously and can sometimes become rather critical, with such high standards that no one can measure up to them. They are devoted to their family and to close friends.

expression number This person sets a lot of store by appearances. They want to give a good impression and they like to be thought of as successful and worldly. They live life to the full and can be quite hedonistic in the process. Stinting themselves is not in their nature! Unpleasant scenes are something they avoid, and they are careful to avoid trouble, too. They are very easy-going but sometimes tend to be rather self-centred.

heart number Happy relationships come easily to this person, partly because they are so eager to please. They want to be seen as reliable, steadfast and trustworthy, and they usually succeed because they go out of their way to help and support others. They expect the same from people in return, and are hurt when they are disappointed. Their domestic and family life is extremely important to them and they devote a lot of time to creating a restful and peaceful home in which they can feel safe.

This is a mystical number, connected with spirituality, contemplation and philosophy. It has connections with Neptune and the sign of Pisces.

destiny number This person has a strong intuition and should follow their gut instincts, which are usually reliable. They may even be psychic. At the very least, they are sensitive to atmospheres and the moods of the people around them. It is important for them to learn to protect themselves against negative people or situations. Creative and imaginative, they can sometimes allow their mind to run away with them, conjuring up demons. They are certainly born worriers. They need a lot of time to themselves.

personality number Psychic abilities are more than likely for someone with this personality number. They are highly sensitive and attuned to the atmosphere around them. They enjoy paying close attention to their dreams, since these can give vital insight into their life and personality. They are very musical, whether they perform or listen to it. Creativity comes naturally to them and should not be stifled. Even if they are not artistic, they should remember that creativity comes in many forms. At times they need to retreat from the rest of the world.

expression number It can take a while to get to know this person. Initially, their shy manner can make them seem remote and slightly unfriendly, but after you have penetrated their defences you will find them charming, affectionate and intelligent. They have an uncanny knack of putting their finger on the nub of things.

heart number This person has a deep urge to merge with a force that is bigger than themselves. They may call this God or have another name for it, but it will be a guiding factor in their life. They may even choose to lead a contemplative or spiritual existence that separates them from others in some way. This can sometimes cause problems with their relationships, especially if they have dedicated their life to a larger purpose. They are frequently misunderstood and may be considered rather strange by people who do not share their view of the world.

This number is linked with the material world. It is also connected with infinity because the infinity symbol resembles a figure eight lying on its side. It relates to the planet Saturn and the sign of Capricorn.

destiny number   This person is propelled through life by a strong driving force. They need to be respected by others and do not want to let themselves down by appearing to be a failure or second best. Appearances definitely matter! Hard work holds no terrors for them and they will embrace it wholeheartedly if it might lead to a better paid job, an enhanced reputation or an improvement in their status. Sometimes, their close relationships can suffer as a result of their powerful ambitions.

personality number   This is someone who knows what they want out of life and is determined to achieve it. They have something to prove, not only to themselves but also to the rest of the world. They are skilled organizers, excellent at making other people work at their best. Their very high standards often lead to perfectionism, which in turn leads to frustration when they fail to meet their own expectations. Relationships are frequently casualties of this person's ambitions and their need for material success – everything has to take second place to their goals and dreams.

expression number   This person is probably a high-powered member of a business or organization. They are a very hard worker and will put in hours of unpaid overtime if that is the only way to enhance their reputation or keep up with their workload. No one could accuse this person of slacking: if anything, they work too hard and have an over-developed sense of responsibility. They are not always as popular as they imagine, but they are very kind beneath what can sometimes be a self-important exterior.

heart number   Someone with this heart number yearns for success. If they do not receive the recognition they believe they deserve, they can become bitter and angry at the way life has apparently cheated them. They enjoy a high standard of living, partly because they see it as a reflection of their worldly success. In relationships, they are faithful and reliable, but they may struggle to show their vulnerable side. Nevertheless, they excel at being the person who organizes everyone else.

A very spiritual number, nine is linked to vision and perfection. It is connected with the planet Mars and with the signs of Aries and Scorpio.

destiny number This person is skilled at devising brilliant ideas, although their initial enthusiasm may flag long before they get round to putting these ideas into practice, so someone else has to do that for them. Nevertheless, they can achieve a great deal and are very competitive. Despite their enthusiasm for life, they may have had a difficult childhood and have weathered many storms since then. Yet they are never despondent for long and will soon bounce back. They live their life in distinct chapters, perhaps severing links along the way.

personality number You will find that this person is strongly humanitarian and very concerned about working for other people, in a variety of ways. Their job may even be connected with charitable works. They are a visionary but dislike waiting for events to develop in the way they would like. As a result they will be very impatient with anyone who is apparently holding up progress. They enjoy travel.

expression number This person makes a big impact on everyone around them. They are bright, bubbly and terrific company. Luckily, they are so popular that their tendency to be painfully honest is usually forgiven. They can swing between being completely selfless and utterly self-centred. In relationships, they need a partner who will appreciate their need for freedom and independence, and who will not be jealous when they flirt with other people.

heart number This person is consumed with curiosity about the world and has a very analytical attitude to life. They may dream of understanding exactly what makes others tick and can be quite ruthless in their desire to get to the bottom of mysterious situations. This does not go down well with partners, who can get the distinct impression that their every action is being analysed in minute detail. They are very compassionate and loving, and enjoy expressing this side of their personality.

Eleven is the first of the two master numbers. It is related to psychic abilities and spiritual insights and has links with the planet Uranus and the sign of Aquarius.

destiny number This person is a born leader, as you would expect considering that eleven consists of two ones. They have an iron determination to achieve their objectives and are usually successful because they do not give up without a struggle. They have a tremendously powerful personality and can be very charismatic – a quality they should be careful not to exploit in order to get their own way.

personality number Here is an idealist who may have a particular message that they want to broadcast to the rest of the world. If so, they will be helped by their ability to be articulate, charismatic and powerful. They are likely to excel in any career that enables them to communicate with others, so will do well in the media. However, they are not so successful in close relationships, because their ambitions and reforming zeal often take precedence over personal considerations.

expression number Creativity flows through this person's veins and they need to express it. Although they may not realize it, other people are very impressed by their artistry and the apparently effortless way they are able to incorporate it into their life. Usually, their creativity will make them very successful in their chosen field, but occasionally they may fritter away their energies on dreams that will never be realized. They have a strong spiritual belief.

heart number This person dreams of making the world a better place and they will not be deterred from putting this vision into practice. As a result, they are survivors, because they will fight tooth and nail to attain their objectives, even if they have to struggle in the process or make plenty of sacrifices. They also have tremendous self-confidence and self-belief. However, this can come at a price, because they may live on their nerves.

This is the second of the two master numbers, and is connected with perfection. It is linked to the planet Neptune and to the sign of Pisces.

destiny number This person has a tremendous amount of potential that is just waiting to be expressed. They should have no problems in doing this since they are very practical and motivated. However, they can sometimes get caught up in internal struggles that take up a lot of their time and energy. As a result, they may fail to accomplish what they set out to do, although they have more than enough ability. They may come into their own as they get older.

personality number This person wants to do the very best they can, and they usually succeed because they have the necessary motivation and determination. However, they should avoid becoming complacent, which will slow them down at best or trip them up at worst. Their relationships are often slow at getting off the ground because they are hesitant to make an emotional commitment. Nevertheless, once the relationship has become established they will want to make it a success and will be faithful and loyal.

expression number Popular, clever and charming, this person is easily noticed. They may give the impression of being slightly helpless, but they are extremely capable and a very good judge of character. Material success is more than likely for them, provided they can overcome a slight inferiority complex that tells them they are not worthy of it. They are idealistic and have a strong humanitarian streak.

heart number This is someone who has a secret desire for success and longs to get involved in humanitarian activities that will benefit the world in general. They are sufficiently motivated and clever to succeed, but they may become side-tracked and achieve less than they intended. They also tend to take the path of least resistance and to give up whenever the going gets tough. Their relationships bring out a curious mixture of a desire for power and a need for harmony.

choosing a baby's name

Numerology allows you to analyse a baby's name and see whether the personality, expression and heart numbers are harmonious. If the child has already been born, you will have the benefit of working with their destiny number as well, because this will give you essential information about the child's true self. This is an example for a baby girl born on 1 June 2001, with a destiny number of one ($1 + 6 + 2 + 1 = 10$; $1 + 0 = 1$). Her parents wanted to call her Ann Smith, with no middle name:

```
 1                        9
 A   N   N      S   M   I   T   H
     5   5      1   4       2   8
```

This gave a heart number of one ($1 + 9 = 10$; $1 + 0 = 1$) and an expression number of seven ($5 + 5 + 1 + 4 + 2 + 8 = 25$; $2 + 5 = 7$). These go well with the destiny number, because they are all odd. However, the personality number is eight ($1 + 7 = 8$) – not very harmonious. So her parents considered calling her Anne:

```
 1           5           9
 A   N   N   E   S   M   I   T   H
     5   5       1   4       2   8
```

Although the expression number remains the same, because it is taken from the consonants in the name and these have not been altered, the heart and personality numbers will change. But will the change yield all odd or masculine numbers?

The heart number adds up to six ($1 + 5 + 9 = 15$; $1 + 5 = 6$). Therefore, the personality number is four ($7 + 6 = 13$; $1 + 3 = 4$). We still do not have four masculine numbers.

Finally, her parents thought of calling her Annabel:

```
 1       1   5               9
 A   N   N   A   B   E   L      S   M   I   T   H
     5   5       2   3       1   4       2   8
```

This gives her a heart number of seven ($1 + 1 + 5 + 9 = 16$; $1 + 6 = 7$). The expression number is three ($5 + 5 + 2 + 3 + 1 + 4 + 2 + 8 = 30$; $3 + 0 = 3$). So far, so good! The personality number is therefore one ($7 + 3 = 10$; $1 + 0 = 1$). This is the same number as the destiny number, and the other two numbers are also odd. Annabel will be someone with the pioneering spirit of one, tempered by the sensitivity of a seven heart number and the confidence of a three expression number.

divining

Divining, also known as dowsing, is one of the most ancient skills
known to man. It is the art of using a pendulum or another other
object to answer questions that are interpreted according to the
direction of the pendulum's swing. It can also be used to detect
the presence of water and look for lost objects. There is nothing
mystical or otherworldly about this because many water
companies employ dowsers to search for leaks in pipes or to
locate sources of fresh water. Some companies hire dowsers
who work with maps to identify potential sources of oil or
minerals — a process that means the companies do not have to
spend money on fruitless searches. Divining is often used to
detect the sex of chickens, when it is carried out at an

236

astonishing speed. In the same vein, before the advent of ultrasound, divining was used to discover the sex of an unborn child by holding the wife's wedding ring over her stomach.

Divining is a good method of asking a question, provided you phrase it in a way that enables the pendulum to respond sensibly. It can only respond to your question in one of four ways: 'Yes', 'No', 'Silly question' and 'Search' when it is locating a lost object. Since the pendulum does not offer any other options it is important to phrase your question in a way that can be answered easily with 'Yes' or 'No'. This is explained in more detail later in this chapter.

It is easy to become accustomed to using a pendulum. In fact, it is one of the simplest techniques in this book. Over the years a great deal of research has been conducted into the use of pendulums, notably by the English scientist TC Lethbridge, who experimented with different lengths of string when asking particular questions. Some of these experiments involved extremely long pieces of string, but there is no need to go to such trouble yourself. A simple pendulum suspended from a reasonable length of cord will work very well.

choosing a pendulum

You can use a variety of different objects as a pendulum, provided you have some way of attaching it to a cord or piece of string. You can buy a traditional brass pendulum, that is shaped like a plumb bob, and already has a cord attached to it. Many shops now sell crystal pendulums that you can wear around your neck when not using them to answer your questions. You can buy a simple rock crystal pendulum, or one made from a particular crystal, that is suitable for your Sun sign or contains healing qualities. Alternatively, of course, you can buy one simply because you like it.

If you are looking for something more unusual, try a heavy ring, a pendant, a stone with a hole in it or even a household object. But whatever you choose, make sure that it is heavy enough to swing properly from the string or cord to which it is attached. Do not suspend a pendulum from a length of ribbon because its flat surface will interfere with the motion of the pendulum. If the pendulum is very lightweight it will not perform properly, and will be blown off-course by even the smallest puff of wind. You also need to ensure the hole in the pendulum is dead centre, otherwise you will not get an even swing.

what is the question?

It is vital to ask your question in a way that enables the pendulum to respond. You will only get 'Silly question' responses if you ask multiple-choice questions. For instance, the pendulum cannot answer 'Yes' or 'No' when you ask, 'Should I go on holiday to Spain or Italy?' and will reply, 'Silly question'. Make your first question 'Should I go on holiday to Spain?', and your second 'Should I go on holiday to Italy?' The pendulum will then be able to answer you. Sometimes you will get the 'Silly question' response when your question seems eminently sensible. This may be because the pendulum is not co-operating with you (in which case, try again) or it could be because the question is irrelevant for reasons that are not yet known to you. Perhaps the question has already been answered?

training your pendulum

Before you are able to use your pendulum to answer questions, you must train it. It will not automatically respond with clear-cut 'Yes' and 'No' answers and you will have to teach it to do so. It is at this point that you will start to view your pendulum not as an inanimate object but as a trustworthy partner giving accurate answers to your questions, provided you are both speaking the same language. Each time you use your pendulum, you must check its responses before asking a question. It will be very misleading if you think the pendulum's clockwise swing always says 'Yes', only to have it answer 'Yes' one day with what is normally its 'No' response.

When you are ready to begin training your pendulum, hold the string loosely between your thumb and forefinger so that the pendulum can swing freely. Keep your other fingers tucked out of the way to avoid them coming into contact with the swinging cord. Resist the temptation to influence the pendulum's swing subtly by moving your arm in the desired direction! Now ask the pendulum to show you a 'Yes' response. You can ask this either mentally or out loud. Continue to concentrate on this request, asking it again if that will help you to remain focused. Start swinging the pendulum and watch carefully to see what happens.

The pendulum will settle into a distinct movement that differs from the original direction in which it swung. For instance, it might begin swinging in a clockwise direction, and then settle into a backwards and forwards motion. Stop the pendulum and ask it the question again. If you are fortunate, the pendulum will repeat its movement. If the pendulum changes the direction of its swing, you will have to be firm with it. You must show it who is boss! Ask it again to show you its 'Yes' response. Continue until you get the same response each time you ask the question.

Now it is time to work on the 'No' response. Hold the pendulum as before, but this time ask it to show you its 'No' answer. This must be a very different swing from the 'Yes' answer so that there is no confusion over the two responses. Repeat the process that you followed for the 'Yes' answer until both you and the pendulum agree on its 'No' response.

Do not be intimidated by people telling you that everyone has to use a particular response for 'Yes', and a particular response for 'No'. The pendulum does not work like this. For instance, my pendulum always swings backwards and forwards for 'Yes' and diagonally for 'No'. Yours may give you an anticlockwise swing for 'Yes' and a sideways one for 'No'. In addition to the 'Yes' and 'No' responses, you need two more – 'Search' and 'Silly question'. 'Search' is often a wide swing and 'Silly question' is often an idle, dithery sort of swing. Ask the pendulum, as before, to show you these responses.

When you are confident about using your pendulum, take things one step further by asking it to change its response mid-swing. Begin by asking it to give you the 'Yes' response, then ask it to change to a 'No' response, and back again. You will soon establish a good working relationship with your pendulum. Ideally, you should practise with your pendulum for several days before being ready to use it as a divination tool. In the meantime, continue to refine your skills by asking it questions to which you already know the answer. For instance, you could hold it over a glass of water and ask it if there is water in the glass. Then ask it a question to which the answer should be 'No', such as whether the glass contains mud.

Before you begin a session in which you will be asking the pendulum questions, go through all the responses to make sure that you know what they are. You may find that the responses change from day to day, although they will remain constant within a particular session. So what was 'Yes' on Thursday may be 'No' on Friday before reverting to 'Yes' again on Sunday. This does not matter, provided that you remember to check in advance so that there is no doubt about what each response means.

training your thoughts

To use your pendulum most effectively, it is not enough to train it to answer your questions. You must also train your mind to concentrate on the questions that you are asking. You may get plenty of 'Silly question' responses if you ask the pendulum a question and then immediately allow your thoughts to drift in another direction, such as whether to have cake with your coffee. In extreme circumstances, you could get the answer to the cake question rather than the one you thought you had asked.

You must also train yourself to switch off from any emotionally charged questions in case your response affects the pendulum. For instance, if you want to ask whether your beloved will marry you, you are unlikely to remain completely calm while you wait for the pendulum to answer. You will have to distract yourself if you want to be given an objective answer, and the best way to do this is to fill your mind with some form of 'white' noise. The dowser Sig Lonegren suggests repeating 'I wonder what the answer will be?' to drown out such as thoughts 'Please say "Yes"!'

how does it work?

The jury is still out on this question although there are several theories, including the idea that some form of radar connection is operating between the pendulum and the dowser. One of the most popular ideas is that your subconscious already knows the answer to your question, so infinitesimal messages from your brain are transmitted down your arm and into your fingers affecting the swing of the pendulum.

Rather than worry about how and why it works, simply tell yourself that it does. The moment you decide that it is all a figment of your imagination or mere wishful thinking, you have reduced the pendulum's power. If you tell yourself that it does not work, you will find that statement to be true. If you tell yourself that it does work, it will. If you start to entertain doubts or listen to someone who pooh-poohs the entire process, it may help to remember that water companies and oil conglomerates are unlikely to waste their precious funds on a technique that does not work.

working with the pendulum

When you are ready to begin work with the pendulum, you will find many different uses for it. You can ask it questions connected with your future, such as 'Will I find a better paid job this month?' or 'Will Deborah telephone me tomorrow?' Try to be as specific as possible when asking your question so that the pendulum knows exactly what is involved, and can respond accordingly. For instance, if you simply ask 'Will I find a better-paid job?', the pendulum might be unable to answer because you have not specified a time frame. Alternatively, it might say 'Yes' but you will be disappointed because you will have to wait a year for this answer to come true. As you become more familiar with your pendulum you will develop a good working relationship with it. Practice may not make perfect, but it definitely helps.

Once you appreciate the power of the pendulum you will not want to restrict it to answering questions about the future. You can also use it to locate lost objects. For instance, if you know your wallet is somewhere in the house but cannot remember where you left it, you can ask the pendulum to help. One way to do this is to put it in the 'search' position and walk through each room in the house until it gives a 'Yes' response. Alternatively you can sit with the pendulum and ask it a systematic series of questions ('Is my wallet in the kitchen?', 'Is my wallet in the sitting room?' and so on) until it tells you which room contains the wallet. You can then walk round the room with the pendulum in 'search' until it says 'Yes'. You should then find your wallet.

You may find that you are better at some pendulum techniques than others. You might have great success when asking the pendulum questions about the future but be less successful when locating lost objects, or vice versa. This is quite normal and is no reflection on your dowsing abilities. Simply respect the pendulum for what it can offer you, and enjoy your relationship with it.

tasseomancy

The art of reading tea leaves, or tasseomancy, is no longer as popular as it once was. This has nothing to do with its accuracy, which can be uncanny, and everything to do with the so-called conveniences of modern society. If you always use tea bags you will never be able to read the tea leaves at the bottom of your cup. Equally, if you always drink instant coffee you will not be able to read your coffee grounds.

Tasseomancy is an art that originated many centuries ago in China. In the East, it has always been believed that bells can drive out evil. A tradition developed of looking inside bells for omens. Gradually, tea cups, with their bell-like shape, came to be regarded as oracles too, and the art of tea leaf reading was born. Reading tea leaves became popular in the West after the introduction of tea in the eighteenth century. Tea was an extremely expensive luxury at the time, and tea caddies even had locks to prevent servants stealing the precious leaves. One can imagine a bored young lady idly swirling the tea dregs

This shape resembles a key, suggesting change is on the way.

around in the bottom of her cup and hoping to see signs of a forthcoming, glittering marriage.

Tasseomancy is a very simple predictive art. It requires little in the way of tools. All you need is a pot of freshly made leaf tea, a cup and a saucer. Leave the tea strainer in the drawer because it will defeat the object of the exercise! Equally, you need a tea pot that allows plenty of tea leaves to flow through the spout. Ideally, there should be no filter at the base of the spout. For the most effective readings, choose a good quality brand of leaf tea. Some of the cheaper varieties consist of diced leaves that form sullen clumps at the bottom of your cup and refuse to co-operate further. You need fairly large leaves, and may get better results with China rather than Indian tea. Keemun is a good choice. Japanese tea is not suitable because the leaves are too long and large. Be prepared to experiment until you find the best tea for your purposes.

When reading coffee grounds, it is best to make the coffee in a large pot and to let the contents settle before pouring. A cafétière will prevent most of the coffee grounds being poured into your cup. As with tea, you will probably have to experiment before finding the best ground coffee for your purposes. For instance, you may find that your favourite brand of coffee does not give the best results. Turkish or Greek coffee is an excellent choice because it is made from fine powder.

choosing a suitable cup and saucer

It is important to choose a cup that helps your reading. Since you will be studying the inside of the cup, it should be as plain as possible – a pattern will confuse you. Ideally, the inside of the cup should be white. Do not use a fluted cup because the tea leaves will become trapped within the curves. It is also essential that you use a cup with a handle, as this is an integral part of the reading. If you want to make the entire experience special, choose an attractive tea pot and beautiful cups and saucers, though tasseomancy can be just as accurate with the contents of your afternoon cup of tea. If you are sharing a pot of tea with someone, the first cup is traditionally poured for the person having the reading. If you both want to read your tea cups, you can bend tradition rather than brewing up another pot.

the tasseomancy ritual

You do not have to follow this traditional ritual but, as with all rituals, it can help you to prepare mentally for what will follow.

When you have drunk the contents of your cup and no more than a teaspoonful of liquid remains (otherwise you will inadvertently wash out your cup), you are ready to begin. For the best results, you must concentrate on what you are doing.

Take the cup in your right hand and hold it by the handle. Swirl the liquid around the cup three times, in an anti-clockwise circle, and then transfer the cup to your left hand and quickly invert it over the saucer. Alternatively, you can place the saucer over the top of the cup and then invert them both. Wait a few minutes to let all the liquid drain out, otherwise the tea leaves or coffee grounds may move when you pick up the cup. You are now ready to begin your reading.

the positions of the symbols in the cup

Each section of the cup has a particular significance. The handle represents the questioner – the person having the reading – so any leaves or grounds in this area of the cup will refer to him or her, rather than to anyone else. The rim of the cup represents the present or the near future. The middle section of the cup rules events that will happen fairly quickly, and the bottom of the cup represents the far future.

Take your time examining the shapes left by the tea leaves or coffee grounds. It takes practice to be able to interpret what may at first look like nothing more than a jumble of indecipherable blobs. Allow your intuition to guide you. It may also help to squint at the shapes so that you see their overall outlines rather than what may be distracting individual details. A trail of tea leaves or coffee grounds indicates a

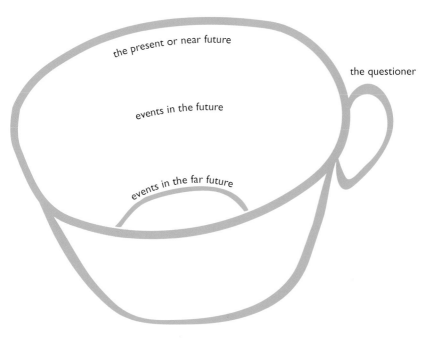

the present or near future

the questioner

events in the future

events in the far future

journey. The stronger this line, the more likely it is that the journey will take place.

A directory of common symbols starts on page 249. It will give you a good base to work from, though it is quite likely that you will encounter other symbols not mentioned here. In that case, start by considering the literal meaning of the object you have seen in the cup as that will give you clues about its symbolism. But do not assume that the literal interpretation is the only one. For instance, if you can see the shape of a violin it may not necessarily mean you should start learning the instrument. Think about what a violin symbolizes. Music is played at celebrations, so it could indicate a party. Music is creative, so the violin might be telling you to develop your artistic gifts. If your question concerns a budding relationship with someone much older than you, the violin may be reminding you that many a good tune is played on an old fiddle. Alternatively, since another name for the violin is the fiddle, this reading may suggest that someone is being dishonest. Let your intuition guide you in the right direction.

There will usually be more than one shape in the cup. Start by interpreting the largest shape, go on to the next largest, and so on. Once you get the hang of it you will find you can marry the meanings of the symbols rather than interpreting them as entirely separate entities. One symbol may moderate the meaning of another.

ceromancy

Scrying, the art of telling the future using wax and a bowl of
water, is centuries old. We have examples of it dating as far back
as the ancient civilizations of Greece and Egypt, although it may
have existed long before then. Babylonian magicians used tablets
to help them interpret the shapes created by pouring melted
wax into water. So when you practise ceromancy you are
continuing a technique that has lasted for thousands of years.

One of the greatest charms of ceromancy is its simplicity. The
only equipment needed is a large candle, a box of matches and a
bowl of cold but not iced water. In addition, you need patience
since you must allow the candle to burn for long enough to
produce a good quantity of melted wax.

In these days of modern electric lighting we tend to think of candles as something special. We light them to create an atmosphere or to set a mood. We put candles on birthday cakes, make a wish and then blow them out again. Yet electricity is only a relatively recent invention, so for thousands of years candles were an essential part of daily life. In a way, we are missing out now that we have so many modern conveniences. One can imagine young girls of the past eagerly taking it in turns to pour the melted wax from a guttering candle into a bowl of water, so that they could discover their future.

choosing your equipment

Although ceromancy is a very simple technique, you need to choose the right equipment in order to get the best results. Choose a large candle because it must burn for at least one hour before you can use the melted wax for ceromancy. That is because you need a generous supply of liquid wax to get a good result. If you only use a small amount the wax will form loops, rather than solid shapes, when tipped into the water.

Choose the colour of the candle carefully. It can be difficult to interpret the shapes of wax from white candles, especially if the inside of the bowl is light in colour. Some people like to use black candles while others have an instinctive antipathy to them, so this is entirely a matter of choice. Since it is traditional to ask a question before tipping the wax into the water, so you may wish to match the colour of the candle with the nature of the question. For instance, you might choose a red or pink candle for matters of the heart, green for health, gold for finance, and so on. If you want to ask several questions relating to different areas of life, burn one candle of each colour at the same time so that they will all be ready when you need them or the process will take hours!

casting the wax

When the candle has been burning for at least one hour, fill a large bowl with cold, but not iced, water. Make sure that the colour of the bowl's interior forms a strong contrast with the colour of the candle, otherwise you won't see a thing! Ideally, you should avoid patterned or raised surfaces because they will make it difficult to read the wax shapes. Ask your question silently or out loud and then pour the melted wax into the bowl. You may prefer to blow out the candle first, to avoid singeing yourself with the flame. You should also take care not to spill the hot wax on your fingers.

Make sure that you pour the wax into the water in the right spirit, and do not allow yourself to be distracted. Keep a sense of the ceremonial aspects of candles. While you are waiting for the

wax to set, keep your mind on your question. Try not to let your thoughts wander because this may make you less receptive to the messages contained in the shape of the wax; it is important to concentrate.

When you are confident that the wax has set, you can start to interpret the shape it has made. You use exactly the same imaginative and intuitive process as when interpreting tea leaves or coffee grounds. For instance, if the wax looks like a shapeless blob, patiently study it from all angles with a clear mind and see which images gradually come to you. If you believe you are looking at the shape of a tree, note that it may not exactly resemble a tree and may have a part missing; your imagination will have to fill in the gaps. If you want to pick the wax out of the water to study it further, handle it very carefully because it will be fragile and could easily crack. Make absolutely sure that the wax has set before you pick it up or the molten wax will spill, and change the shape of what you are looking at.

When you are ready to interpret the wax shape, turn to the directory which begins opposite. Since the meaning of a shape produced by ceromancy will not differ from the meaning of one produced by tasseomancy, this directory applies to both techniques.

If you want to use ceromancy as a divination technique for other people, you will feel most confident if you practise on yourself first. You will then feel more at ease with the entire process, and also with interpreting the wax shapes in the water.

directory of shapes

Here are interpretations of some of the shapes you may see when practising tasseomancy (see pages 242–245) or ceromancy (pages 246–248). Remember to view the shapes from different angles and use your intuition when interpreting them.

 Acorn The start of a new venture or the germ of an idea. It is especially favourable at the top of the cup.

Aeroplane A journey. If the aeroplane is pointing downwards, it can indicate a disappointment or hopes dashed.

Anchor A journey by sea. If it appears at the bottom of the cup it can show that you feel held back by something or someone.

Angel Someone in your life will be very helpful. Good news in love.

Apple Things are looking up. It can also symbolize the attainment of knowledge. Sometimes it can indicate a temptation.

Arch You will be moving from one situation to another. An arch can foretell a journey.

Arrow A letter brings bad news.

Axe A difficulty or argument. If the axe has no handle, you are facing an impossible task.

Baby or foetus (*right*) The start of a new venture or creative project. Sometimes, it means the birth of a child.

 Ball A project is gathering momentum. Occasionally it means being mown down by the opposition.

 Balloon A difficulty is only temporary.

Basket If full, this shows a gift or good fortune. Sometimes it shows the birth of a child. If empty, you will lack something.

 Bed You need to rest. If accompanied by a star or heart, it shows a happy relationship.

 Bee A busy and productive time.

 Bell Unexpected news. Two bells indicate a wedding.

 Bird(s) If the birds are in flight, good news will soon be on the way. Dots around a bird indicate scandal.

 Birdcage A feeling of being trapped if the door is closed. If the door is open, a difficulty will soon be over.

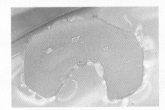

Boat (*above*) This can either mean a short journey or it symbolizes being bailed out in time of trouble, especially if it is at the bottom of the cup.

 Book The acquisition of knowledge. If the book is closed, it can represent represent secret information. If open, a new chapter will soon begin.

Boomerang What goes around comes around – you will soon experience the consequences of recent actions, good or bad.

Bouquet A very favourable sign denoting celebration, happiness and gifts. It can indicate marriage.

Box A gift.

Bridge An opportunity will lead to something new and successful.

Broom It is time to clear the decks of something.

Butterfly Transformation and major change. If accompanied by difficult symbols it can indicate someone who is unfaithful or unreliable.

Cake A celebration.

Candle Marking time.

 Car Short journeys. Visits from friends.

 Chain Strong emotional ties.

 Chair You will soon be in a new position. It can indicate promotion.

 Chimney Plans are about to go up in smoke.

Church A legacy. It can also mean taking a vow, but not necessarily one connected with marriage.

 Claw Someone is not as friendly as they seem.

 Clock Look for any numbers that will indicate time. If the clock is near the rim of the cup it shows time being wasted. At the bottom of the cup it can sometimes mean severe illness.

 Clouds Problems lie ahead. If surrounded by dots, there are financial worries.

 Coat A break or ending in a relationship.

 Comet Unexpected and sudden events.

 Corkscrew Dishonesty.

 Crab Be wary of false friends. Trust your intuition.

 Crescent The start of something new.

Crown Success and achievement. This could represent promotion or a better job. It can also indicate being in the public eye.

 Cup Happiness and emotional fulfilment. If it is overturned, it shows the end of a relationship.

 Dagger Be wary of false friends.

Dog A faithful friend. If the dog is begging, it indicates that help is needed.

 Door One area of life is coming to an end and another will soon begin.

 Dove A harmonious relationship.

 Dragon Do not be afraid to be your true self, no matter who or what that is.

 Drum Important news. A good time to express an opinion.

 Ear Listen carefully because you will hear something to your advantage.

 Egg New plans and schemes stand a good chance of being a success. A birth, whether literal or metaphorical. When timing events, an egg can sometimes represent Easter.

 Egg cup A minor problem is now passing.

 Eye Be alert and watchful in case someone is trying to deceive you. Do not believe everything you see.

 Face(s) A smiling face shows happiness. An unpleasant face shows an adversary. Several faces indicate a social event.

 Fan A flirtatious relationship.

 Feet You need to reach a decision.

 Finger The finger itself does not mean anything, but what is it pointing at? If it points at nothing, a plar will fizzle out.

 Fireplace Home and home comforts. Emotional warmth.

 Flag Danger – be alert.

 Fly Petty irritations. A snag in an otherwise happy situation.

Fork Someone is not to be trusted because they are not telling the truth.

 Forked path A new opportunity will soon arrive.

 Fruit Prosperity and good fortune.

 Glass You feel fragile and are easily hurt. It can also indicate someone whose motives are transparent. More than one glass indicates a celebration.

Grapes You can turn a talent into money.

 Guitar A harmonious relationship.

 Gun There will be quarrels. Possible danger.

 Hammer You need to make your point strongly and forcefully.

 Hand A faithful lover or reliable friend. If the hand is clenched it shows a quarrel or vendetta.

 Handcuffs These can mean legal problems. They can also show an addiction or an enslavement to someone or something.

 Hat Traditionally, this means a gift. You may discover more according to the type of hat it is. For instance, a jester's hat may indicate the need to pretend to be something you are not.

 Head You will soon be given a position of authority.

Heart Indicates long-lasting affection and love.

 Horseshoe Tremendous good fortune!

 Hourglass Do not procrastinate over important tasks.

 House A very favourable sign. It can indicate several things – a house move, being happy at home or a time to start new projects.

R **Initial letter** This is often the initial letter of someone who is important to you. Alternatively, it may be the first letter of a country that has a lot of significance for you or which you will soon be visiting.

 Jug An indication of good health. It can also show happy times with friends.

 Key Changes are on the way, often linked to an opportunity.

 Knife A disagreement may lead to a broken relationship.

 **Ladder** Your circumstances are changing for the better. Possible job promotion.

 Lamp You will uncover a mystery or shed light on an old problem. Sometimes a lamp can indicate a course of formal education.

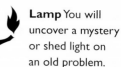 **Leaves** Something in your life is flourishing. Several leaves show great happiness.

Lines A journey. Wavy lines can denote indecision.

 Lion Strength in adversity. You have more courage than you realize.

Lock (*right*) Something is opening for you, such as an opportunity, or closing, such as a relationship.

 Magnifying glass A good time to concentrate on details.

 Man A visitor. If his arm is outstretched, he brings a gift or an opportunity.

 Medal Your achievements will be rewarded.

 Monkey Someone is being mischievous or dishonest.

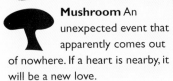 **Mushroom** An unexpected event that apparently comes out of nowhere. If a heart is nearby, it will be a new love.

 Numbers These are a good indication of time. For instance, the number two at the base of the cup might mean two months; it could mean two weeks when in the middle, and two days when on the rim. Numbers can also refer to amounts of money.

 Owl Either illness or betrayal by a friend.

Padlock When it is open, this indicates a surprise. When closed, it carries a warning.

 Parachute A lucky escape from an accident or difficulty. It warns against recklessness.

 Parcel A gift or surprise package.

 Pear Something comes to successful fruition. It can indicate a happy love affair.

 Pickaxe It will take determination to overcome obstacles, but do not be too forceful.

 Purse A gain of some kind. If the purse is surrounded by dots, the gain will be financial.

 Pyramid Are you worried about something that you have to keep a secret? A pyramid can also indicate feeling torn between spiritual and material desires.

Question mark Indecision and uncertainty.

Ring Engagement or marriage, or some other emotional commitment. If dots are nearby, it is a business partnership.

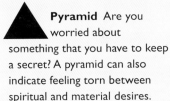

Rocks Difficulties lie ahead. If other symbols are fortunate, these obstacles will be navigated safely.

Scales Some form of balance is needed, according to the way the scales are tipping. They can indicate a lawsuit, especially if accompanied by a sword.

Scissors A serious or far-reaching misunderstanding.

Shamrock Great good fortune. The attainment of something very rare and precious.

Shell Good news.

Ship A happy and successful journey. It can also refer to a significant dream.

Snail Take things slowly and do not rush into hasty decisions.

Spectacles You will soon see something from a completely new perspective.

Spider Money is on the way.

Square Stability and comfort. However, there may be a tendency towards complacency.

Star A wish will come true.

Steeple This denotes a church. It indicates a wedding or a religious vocation.

Steps Success and promotion. You are going up in the world!

Sun Happiness, contentment and creativity. Possibly the birth of a child.

Telephone An important message is on the way. It can sometimes indicate that you are not yet ready to tell someone what you think.

Tent An adventurous journey. It can also show that something is being hidden from you.

Torch Enlightenment and knowledge.

Umbrella If open, there will be difficulties. If closed, be prepared for problems.

Volcano Something is about to erupt. You may have to control your emotions.

Weathervane Indecision. You are swayed by other people's opinions and their expectations of you, and need to gain some objectivity.

Wheel This always describes the cycle of life. A chapter is ending and a new one is beginning. If an obstacle is blocking the wheel, it shows you need to remove the hurdles that stand in the way of progress.

Window You need to view a problem or relationship in a different way. Someone may help you to do this.

index